EMOTIONAL INTELLIGENCE

The Complete Psychologist's Guide to Mastering Social Skills

(A Step-by-step Guide for Beginners to Increase Eq Skills)

Daniel Templeton

Published by

Daniel Templeton

All Rights Reserved

Emotional Intelligence: The Complete Psychologist's Guide to Mastering Social Skills (A Step-by-step Guide for Beginners to Increase Eq Skills)

ISBN 978-1-77485-235-4

All rights reserved. No part of this guide may be reproduced in any form without permission in writing from the publisher except in the case of brief quotations embodied in critical articles or reviews.

Legal & Disclaimer

The information contained in this book is not designed to replace or take the place of any form of medicine or professional medical advice. The information in this book has been provided for educational and entertainment purposes only.

The information contained in this book has been compiled from sources deemed reliable, and it is accurate to the best of the Author's knowledge; however, the Author cannot guarantee its accuracy and validity and cannot be held liable for any errors or omissions. Changes are periodically made to this book. You must consult your doctor or get professional medical advice before using any of the suggested remedies, techniques, or information in this book.

Upon using the information contained in this book, you agree to hold harmless the Author from and against any damages, costs, and expenses, including any legal fees potentially resulting from the application of any of the information provided by this guide. This disclaimer applies to any damages or injury caused by the use and application, whether directly or indirectly, of any advice or information presented, whether for breach of contract, tort, negligence, personal injury, criminal intent, or under any other cause of action.

You agree to accept all risks of using the information presented inside this book. You need to consult a professional medical practitioner in order to ensure you are both able and healthy enough to participate in this program.

Table of Contents

INTRODUCTION 1

CHAPTER 1: THE HABITS OF SELF-AWARENESS AWARENESS 3

CHAPTER 2: EMOTIONAL INTELLIGENCE REVEALED 11

CHAPTER 3: BUILDING AND MANAGING EMOTIONS 31

CHAPTER 4: START WITH HONEST SELF-APPRAISAL 44

CHAPTER 5: WHAT ARE EMOTIONS AND HOW CAN THEY INFLUENCE US AND OUR PERFORMANCE 58

CHAPTER 6: THE EATING REGIMEN 74

CHAPTER 7: THE SOCIAL PROBLEMS THAT AFFECT CHILDREN 91

CHAPTER 8: YOU CAN CHANGE YOUR MINDSET 101

CHAPTER 9: CONTROLLING YOUR EMOTIONS 108

CHAPTER 10: TIPS TO FIND EMOTIONAL CONTROL AND TACKLE ANGER MANAGEMENT 116

CHAPTER 11: THE PRACTICES OF TRANSFORMATIONAL LEADERS 124

CHAPTER 12: EMOTIONAL INTELLIGENCE 131

CHAPTER 13: WHAT HAPPENS IF WE DO NOT MAKE TIME FOR RECOVERY? 141

CHAPTER 14: WHAT IS EMOTIONAL INTELLIGENCE? 145

CHAPTER 15: THE PRIMARY EMOTIONS OF PLUTCHIK ... 158

CHAPTER 16: THE TOOLS TO CONTROL YOUR EMOTIONS 163

CHAPTER 17: THE BUILDING BLOCKS OF EMOTIONAL INTELLIGENCE 167

CHAPTER 18: WHAT MAKES AN EMOTIONALLY STRONG AND INTELLIGENT PERSON? 178

CONCLUSION 185

Introduction

Over the past 10 years it has gained more and more recognition around throughout the world.In the book below, we're going to discuss the subject of emotional intelligence, and provide you a brief overview and the steps you can take to increase your level in emotional intelligence. One of the major benefits to the concept of emotional intelligence is the research results that show it is that intelligence quotient (IQ) isn't as significant for us as our emotional quotient (EQ) is. It's been demonstrated that only 20 percent of "common" intelligence-related responses contribute to our many accomplishments and achievements as the other 20% are based on emotional intelligence. Research has shown that intellect isn't enough to be able to achieve success in life. You'll be awestruck by how effective your emotional intelligence can be in relation with academic achievement, social abilities, and leadership. I hope you be able to benefit from the knowledge gathered in this book on the subject of emotion intelligence within this publication and will find it useful to you to develop your skills and emotional intelligence.

Chapter 1: The habits of Self-awareness Awareness

Self-awareness is an essential component of emotional intelligence because it allows you to identify mood emotions, emotions, and emotions. It is essential to recognize them as it will enable you to manage them and tame the bad ones.

These are the traits which show how confident and skilled people are with their personal emotions.

1. Pay attention to how they feel.

The most emotionally intelligent people don't avoid feeling what they are experiencing because they realize that what is lingering inside them may become too painful or insufferable to contain. They are attentive because they wish to block out negative emotions that can still be contained. However they wish to savor every bit of their positive feelings for as long as they can.

Application: Don't ignore those negative feelings because they'll return if left unsolved. Also, not taking advantage of every moment of the wonderful feelings you feel is wasting the chance to relax and improve your self-love.

2. They completely understand their emotions.

They don't have to doubt the way they feel since they're attuned to their own inner self. They are always trying to determine the meaning behind what they feel. an excellent or negative issue because the choice they must take is contingent on the feeling. When there is confusion they take the time to analyze their feelings and decide on what they would like to resolve it.

Application Emotional confusion is the initial stage that leads to mental delusions. To be confident in your own abilities and making the right decisions it is important to understand the real feelings you feel in specific situations.

3. They pinpoint what causes them emotional problems.

Everyone hopes to find inner happiness and peace in their lives however, people who are emotionally intelligent put in extra effort to tackle the issue. The first step is to remove the causes and triggers for their emotional problems. They identify these as excess baggage that do not affect their development.

Application: If you already know your feelings Think about the things or people that cause you to be uneasy, agitated, unsure or insecure. They can make you feel frightened, angry overwhelmed, frustrated, and unhappy. Be sure to stay clear of them as best you can. Consider the things which make you feel relaxed, peaceful, secure and happy. Find them and ensure that you've got them around especially in tough times.

4. They are able to match their emotions to the right amount of energy.

They make a conscious effort to display the energy that is equivalent to their emotions. They limit their energy whenever they are feeling down to prevent angry outbursts, but they also have more energy when they feel happy to express their joy, which can result in an infectious disease. Achieving the appropriate amount of energy is essential to avoid the transmission of an untrue message.

Application: Manage the energy you invest in each emotion you feel. It shouldn't be a problem to appear aggressive. This could help you avoid infuriating other people in addition. This shouldn't be too small to be sure you convey exactly what you wish to convey. It isn't a good idea to let people continue to harass and abuse you , since you are unable to express frustration or anger, similarly, you do not want people to believe that you're unworthy because you aren't displaying the happiness and contentment you deserve.

5. They are responsible for the consequences of their actions and actions.

The idea of blaming others for how they do and think is not a good idea since ultimately it is they that control their own thoughts, feelings and their actions. They know that, and so they examine themselves as to why they feel and think like they do rather than asking others what made them think and feel the way they do.

Application: Control your feelings and behavior to avoid hurting your self and others. Little things shouldn't be exacerbated by overreacting in retaliation since damaged relationships are very difficult to fix. Make changes to the way you respond first before you attempt to change the people that are causing you to react badly.

6. They recognize the inevitable changes that will occur in their control of their emotions.

They aren't averse to changes in their perspective and coping strategies because they realize the need to develop and become more mature in managing their emotions. They accept changes that improve their lives however they reject the ones that other people have created to profit from their strengths. They trust their conscience and change their behavior.

Application: Once you've identified the new habits you'll need to make, take them on with all your heart, no matter if they're difficult or easy since you are trying to be more emotionally intelligent.

7. They can improve their weaknesses in emotional expression and tap into their strengths as emotional.

They recognize the elements of their personalities that require improvements, like their temperament or patience, as well as the qualities which they have to utilize to stand out as their joy and compassion. Since they are aware of the factors that make their emotions fragile they are aware and move in the opposite direction as much as they can when confronted with individuals and situations that expose them to their flaws. However they become close to people who highlight their strengths so that they are able to nourish their emotional well-being.

Application: Determine your weaknesses emotionally and think about what causes them to behave that way. Find the root of the issue and find out why you are feeling like this. Look at the ways you could make by putting in greater control.

Additionally, you should show your strengths in emotional areas frequently because they provide you with character. Be calm when there is confusion and chaos about you. Display your joy and optimism in the face of people who are depressed, sad and angry. Your strengths in emotional expression can help one stand out from the group to change the lives of others for the best.

8. They are tolerant of all the good and negative qualities they possess.

They are aware that they must be taught in one way or another. While they're proud of the best attributes, they're not embarrassed by their poor ones, as emotionally intelligent individuals are confident and self-assured about their abilities. They know they will improve and laugh at their mistakes when they reflect at their past.

Application: Be proud of your positive characteristics, but don't sully those that are not so good. You can transform your worst characteristics into an arsenal of emotions if you alter and improve the way you use them. The only time that you should be embarrassed about yourself is when you decide to not take action regarding your flaws in the emotional department.

Chapter 2: Emotional Intelligence Revealed

Intelligence is an incredibly widely-known term. We have created tests to test it, as well as ways to evaluate the results. An intelligence quotient (I.Q.) is typically used to measure the ability of a person to complete various cognitive tasks, including memory recall, maths as well as spatial thinking. The tests are designed to assess a specific aspect of the human brain.

But they do not provide any information about the health of a person or how they deal with the stresses of daily life. This is the place where emotional intelligence comes into the picture. Before getting into its definition, answer these questions to determine what you already know:

1.) You're attending a party that is hosted by a friend. After a while , the atmosphere becomes more relaxed, and your partner who has was drinking a couple of drinks more and decides to share a few embarrassing memories from your past with the guests present at the party. You:

be embarrassed and leave the event the earliest time possible and hope that no one will remember this before the next day.

Participate in the conversation, but shift your focus to the things that your spouse has done in the past.

interrupt the story and request your spouse to come with you to the outside, in a quiet place, where you gently insist that he not share these stories to anyone else.

Make it public that you and your partner has had too much alcohol and is making the claims up.

2.) You're at an office meeting and a colleague gives credit to your work. You:

You must immediately speak to your colleague about the responsibility of your work. You should let everyone know what you have completed.

Wait for the meeting to close and then take your coworker away and tell him or her that you would be grateful in the future that they credit you for the work that you did.

Don't do anything, since it's not good for your career to embarrass or humiliate your colleagues.

You should publicly thank your colleague to reference your work and offer the group more specific information about your thoughts.

3)After having a long day at work, you stop at the closest supermarket. The cashier is naive and charges you too much by adding items you don't need. You:

Don't say anything, pay for your purchases and then leave the shop because you're eager to return back home as soon as you can.

Start disputing with the cashier, and ask to discuss the matter with the supervisor.

Inform the cashier of there was a mistake and ask them to fix it , since you don't require that additional item.

You can pay for the additional item, and then decide that you don't will ever go back to the store because they were clearly trying to trick you into purchasing things you don't require.

4.) You get a call from your boss from home, yelling at you that items are missing from the office and suggests that you stole these items. What should you do?

Simply explain in a calm manner that it's probably not the case that you were very suspicious in the last couple of days.

You are offended and then hang off the phone at the end of the conversation.

After listening to him and trying to figure out the issue, you can offer your assistance to resolve the problem.

Get into a heated argument with him as he's clearly insane to make such a statement in this specific situation. He most likely wants to take the blame for his anger on you.

5) You're in the situation that you have a friend who complains about a common friend's behaviour. What should you do?

You, without thinking, you agree with your friend since evidently s/he requires some peace in this tense situation.

you are listening and trying to offer tips on how you can retaliate to the unfairness that occurred to her or him

If you are listening, but with no opinion, the other side you listen to, try to comprehend the events that transpired and do your best to not bring your personal feelings in the discussion

If you decide to contact a mutual acquaintance to explain what transpired. Everyone should be aware of the shocking incident.

For each one of these social situations that you went through in the short test above There are a variety of possibilities for how you can react. Being aware of how you should respond in a specific social setting as well as how the actions we take impact our interactions with other people is aspect of the social intelligence. It is believed as the capacity to be able to manage and understand the self as well as other people. Furthermore, it's the capacity to maintain positive relationships with others and be able to comprehend the emotions of other people's motivations, behaviors, and motives. Most importantly, it's the capacity to draw upon this understanding of others to guide your own actions and reactions towards other people.

The opposite of this can be described as emotional intelligence (EI). It is part of the social intelligence. It is characterized by our ability to keep track of the emotions and feelings of our own and also the emotions and feelings of other people. In addition, emotional intelligence is the ability to differentiate between these emotions and feelings, and utilize this information to determine our thoughts and actions.

It allows us to effectively communicate with others and to understand their feelings and emotions as than if they were ones. In essence, it is a way of getting to understanding ourselves: our internal state of mind that guide our daily thinking and actions as well as the feelings we experience at the beginning of the day without coffee, or when a coworker receives the raise you hoped for.

Emotional intelligence assists us manage those emotions and feelings and equips us with the mental ability to deal with these emotions. It provides us with the ability to examine the current state of our emotions and apply them to our current circumstances, without allowing them to influence our actions and decisions. In addition, it allows us to realize that most of the time , we are in the grip of emotions and feelings, regardless of whether it is ours or of others who surround us, even if we don't always realize the reality.

The vast array of talents that make up the realm of emotional intelligence can lead to a greater understanding of ourselves as well as the people who surround us. In the long run it can bring more fulfillment to your life. The variety of abilities that comprise emotional intelligence is typically divided into four categories. They include the ability to recognize and recognize emotions; the capability to comprehend emotions; managing emotions, and emotional reasoning.

The ability to detect and recognize emotions

The initial and most crucial step to understanding the emotional intelligence of a person is to recognize emotions in the way they really are. It is essential to understand the person we are, to understand the emotion that is within us at a specific moment. This is not just beneficial for understanding our own emotions however, it can also help us discern the emotions that appear in other people.

Feelings in Yourself

The process of improving our emotional intelligence begins as soon as we start to recognize emotional signals from our surroundings. The ability to recognize emotions helps us correctly and precisely assess the range of emotional states and feelings and how to express these to other people. The most commonly used method to accomplish this is through language.

It is essential to know what's going on at an emotional level, to be able to express what we truly would like to say as well as avoid making mistakes that can result in an uneasy situation. Another method of expressing feelings and thoughts is through non-verbal communication, which includes facial and body language expressions. Understanding yourself and your feelings is crucial to ensure that you are able to communicate effectively and avoid potentially dangerous miscommunications.

People's emotions in other people

The ability to sense and understand emotions in ourselves can help us identify emotions in other people. Once we are aware of what emotion or emotion can be expressed, and what it means, we can recognize it in other people and appropriately react to it.

You've probably gathered from experience, discussing emotions can be difficult or at best difficult to be accurate (which is the reason identifying emotions within ourselves is crucial). That's why it's crucial to understand how to look beyond the words someone employs. The ability to detect the nonverbal expressions of emotion (such such as gestures) is essential to increase your ability to communicate and comprehend emotions.

It is not possible to achieve this by identifying the emotions. It is necessary to be able to discern the emotions you have discovered. You must learn to walk in the shoes of someone else. This is referred to as empathy. It is an essential component that is a part of the emotional intelligence. It aids us in understanding each other better and offers us the chance to assist each other in achieving our goals and grow as people.

The ability to recognize emotions

It isn't always enough since they can have many different meanings. It is crucial to understand what emotions are. If we are feeling either sad or happy, we have to realize that it is likely to be an occasional occurrence. This is definitely helpful in processing the emotions we feel, especially when we are sad.

Furthermore If we awake feeling down in the morning, and our view that the universe around us appears veiled in a gray-colored veil, it is important to realize that the world didn't change overnight, however, this feeling is rooted within our minds and will, as it always happens disappear with the passage of the passage of time. Understanding what triggers us to feel that way can help us address the issue and make the process go faster.

The ability to recognize emotions doesn't just apply to our own, but it also applies to the feelings of other people. For instance, if someone is sad and showing sadness, you'll need to recognize the emotion and determine what the sadness signifies: what led to it and how do you respond to it?

If your spouse is feeling down, after you came back from work, it may not mean that you have done something that might make them feel angry. It could be that they were having a difficult time at work or were saddened by the news of the family member or friend of a member.Again If your boss at work is showing an angry mood, it's not because they're unhappy about your job or perhaps due to an argument with their partner at the beginning of the day prior to going to work.

The ability to discern not just what feelings you're experiencing but also what caused them, and how to best react to them. It will help us not only better understand ourselves but also better manage the emotional state we are in. Learning to read and comprehend the feelings of others will enable us to communicate more effectively and control our responses to avoid conflict.

How to manage emotions

When you explore your knowledge of the mood of others or your own mood, you're in the process of evaluating, monitoring and controlling emotions. Ability to handle your emotions effectively is, therefore, one of the most important aspects of the emotional intelligence. This involves regulating your emotions and emotions on one hand, and being able to respond appropriately to the moods and feelings of other people on the contrary.

How to manage your emotions

The majority of the moods occur in us happen naturally. If we're at funerals, in the depressing atmosphere that comes with the loss of a loved one it is natural to feel sad. But, we are able to manage our emotions and decide what mood we're in. Imagine you're out in the evening on Friday dancing. You're probably feeling energized as well as full of enthusiasm having a blast. Recalling this moment in the future could aid in getting that same sensation.

Similar things happen when you recall an incident you witnessed just a few weeks ago. In addition, the dance can trigger the same emotions that you felt on that Friday night. It is vital to be aware of the circumstance we're in. We don't want anyone to be able to see us dancing at a funeral, for instance.

Another method to control your mood and mood is to choose those we are friends with. Drinking a beverage or eating lunch with people who are positive is likely to cause us to feel positive and content. If it isn't an option and we're in a lonely place, our mood and mood can be altered by deciding to be positive instead of negativity.

When you feel down and depressed that can be painful, many prefer to imagine that their feelings are under control. The feeling of control typically leads to feeling happier and more optimistic.

How to manage emotions in others

The term "emotional intelligence" also refers to the ability to control and control the emotions of other people. For instance an applicant who is successful must be aware of the importance of proper conduct, such as attending the interview on time and dress in a formal attire to create an impression and increase the likelihood of getting employed.

Furthermore, a successful presenter at a business gathering must also be aware of how important it is to know the audience. This can assist him in not only capturing the attention of the audience but also trigger strong emotional reactions to the message. Being emotionally intelligent is having the understanding of how to construct scenes in which specific emotions you desire will be triggered.

In addition, the capacity to discern when it is not necessary to be attentive to the behavior of others is just as crucial as knowing when you need to pay attention. Certain behavior can get worse by acknowledging. If you're parents or have had to look after a child, you are aware that acknowledging a child's rage can make the problem more severe because the primary reason of the act was to attract your attention.

Even among adults there are some behavior patterns (like involuntary threat or outbursts) which are best not to be acknowledged. Understanding how to spot the behaviors that can be remediated more quickly by not ignoring the issue is an important aspect of communicating with those in your life.

Emotional reasoning

The highest level of emotional intelligence refers to your ability to think emotionally. It is the use of emotions to stimulate cognitive thinking and thinking. Instead of believing that your emotions are emotions that are irrational and hinder your ability to think rationally, you need to be aware of two points. It is firstly, it is impossible to take any decision without emotions being involved (no no matter how objective you attempt to be). Second, your emotions could actually assist you in making wise or even beneficial choices.

If people aren't aware of the role that emotions play in our reasoning and reasoning, they are prone to the habit of thinking badly. They might say something like "I am bored at the moment, which means I'm boring." One of the aspects to being an emotionally intelligent person is understanding that the feelings you experience don't reflect your true self-identity as a person. It's more about your response to the circumstances you're in at the moment.

Let's say you are planning an important meeting in the office. It's normal to be somewhat anxious about this occasion. However, if you failed to succeed in the past similar occasion, you're likely to find that you'll start to think about it as a generalization and believe that you'll make the same mistakes in this particular meeting. The result of emotional naivety is that you'll be even more stressed than you ought to be.

It's easy to fall into traps of poor emotional reasoning and make assumptions such as: "I got too nervous and failed the first time, and I'm likely to do the same thing next time." However, the more you believe in this false logic, greater the likelihood that this is to be a self-fulfilling prophecy. If you truly believe that you're going to be unsuccessful, then you most likely will fail.

If you, however you are able to appreciate the positive aspects of your life, you're more likely to be successful. In this instance you could think about how your prior failed experience taught you lots about what you must and shouldn't do. This time around, you'll be better well-prepared for what's about to happen and will have planned more carefully before arriving.

It is possible to be focused on the fact that almost every person is anxious when what they're about to do is crucial to them. That means your anxious feeling indicates that you're doing what you're supposed to do because you're pushing yourself to the edge of your comfort zone to achieve something you would never be able to accomplish had you not pushed yourself to this level. By doing this you're not just admitting your real feelings (nervousness and anxiety about being unsuccessful) but also using them to make sense of the future. These are the thoughts that will drive you to be successful. You can only be scared of failing if are driven to achieve success.

Chapter 3: Building and managing Emotions

Emotional intelligence is the capacity to manage your emotions and apply to enhance our lives. Being aware of how we feel is extremely beneficial since it lets us control our emotions and stress whenever needed. It lets us be able to communicate with others without damaging their impressions or moods.

We're all aware of the concept of what an the intelligence quotient (IQ) is however have you had the opportunity to learn about emotional quote? It is a measure of emotional intelligence. (EQ) is an indicator of the degree to which the level of your personal psychological intelligence is.Considering the fact that our IQs stay constant throughout life, it's an amazing thing to know to know that EQ can be improved with the passage of time and practice. How is this possible?

Building Your Emotional Quotient

Here are a few ways to increase your EQ

Be aware. We need to be able to see the ways in which our actions and emotions are linked. The more we know about our actions and emotions towards particular situations more elevated our EQ is. Therefore, it will help us recognize our emotions and assist us in controlling our reactions in the future. It is important to identify certain reactions that are not intentional that result from some of the emotions that we feel. For example, if you are angry, you shout or typically you raise your fist. If you are embarrassed, you will are withdrawn from your social circle. It is important to understand your feelings and bodily responses, and do all you can to control them both.

Don't be a judge of yourself. Making yourself judged will affect your thinking process and emotions.It can cause you to not express your emotions to yourself. It will cause you to lie to yourself about your feelings. Being able to feel and display emotions is normal and isn't an offense.

However, you need to control the bodily reaction based on your feelings. If you try to keep your emotions in the most basic situations, and then later when you are confronted with an unpredictable circumstance, you'll surprise yourself with an unexpected reaction that nobody is prepared for. Without knowing how your body reacts you would not know how to react! By feeling as well as understanding the emotions you build emotional intelligence.

Find the connections in your personal history. Recognize how you've responded to certain situations during the course of your life. If you examine the connections between your actions and emotions it will allow you to understand how to manage your behavior and emotions when you need to and make better choices. It's like making a model from your personal history of emotions and then studying it to discover which areas of weakness are.In order to accomplish this better, you should record your reactions to certain emotions to ensure that you are able to clearly map the emotional patterns.

Do your best to practice your behaviour. It might sound strange, but it's an effective method. If you are able to spend some time to yourself, let both your negative and positive emotions to emerge at a time. Make an effort to fight negative emotions without reacting with a violent response. Take in all positive emotions and let them be in control. So, you'll discover how to allow the positive and negative emotions to be visible, while the negative emotions won't require a bodily response. That is you'll feel the negative emotion, but you will choose not to react to it.

Be open to the opinions of other people. Do not shut down your mind thinking that your views are the truth. Let everyone else have a little slack and pay attention for what people are saying. You can increase your emotional intelligence simply by becoming more sociable and open. This will give you an understanding of other people who are expressing their feelings and how they react. People with narrow minds usually have a low EQ. An open-minded person typically is able to cope when situations arise and require a clear response.

Become a people person. One of the most important characteristics of someone with an elevated EQ is their capacity to empathize with other people. You must be able to comprehend what people are feeling and assist them to understand and communicate their emotions the presence of others. Keep your ears open in front of people in order to discern clearly how someone feels. You will know that you're becoming more emotionally intelligent when you begin to relate to how others feel and altering your behaviour in line with what you feel. This can be accomplished by placing yourself in other people's shoes, walking for a mile in them, and then being completely attuned to the way they talk and feel.

Pay attention to the body language of people. Learn to read in between the lines so that you understand precisely what you're talking to feels. Be aware of their facial expressions as well as body expressions. Try to be more attentive and connecting their feelings to your own.

Be truthful with yourself. When you make a statement that you truly mean that you mean it. Being transparent with yourself and with others is essential to improving your EQ. This will allow people to trust and believe in your character. They will be able to comprehend the place you're coming from. However, being honest with your emotions doesn't mean you have to expose all of your emotions, positive or negative in public. It could harm your reputation and the reputation of your colleagues.

Ask yourself questions. Ask yourself questions such as "Why? What? Where? What time? What?" Questioning yourself will help you think about your actions and ask questions about their legitimacy. This will assist you in managing your future actions. When you are done with the day, when you're getting ready to close your eyes and retire to bed take a moment to reflect on every action and ask yourself "Why did I behave in this way?" Notice and realize all the external factors that led you to react to the way you did. Ask yourself questions like:

"What did I think?"

"What else could have done in that particular situation?"

"Why did I feel so in that moment?"

"Was I acting in a way that was irrational?"

"Was this act a possibility to stop?"

When your mind begins to question your beliefs, you'll begin to distinguish between rights and wrongs, and you can make the right decision.

Get a lesson from critics. Yes, criticism hurts. It can make people feel vulnerable, and vulnerable. It is never a good idea to hear things about ourselves that are negative from anyone, regardless of how close they may be to us.When people make comments about your character, they will expose your worst characteristics. Only after your shortcomings are exposed, are you able to recognize your weaknesses and the necessity for improvement. If we think that we're perfect and it is not "changeable" regarding us we're not right. It is important to search for people who are known to be honest with us and we should keep in touch with them since they've identified our weaknesses and can help us comprehend our emotions more clearly. We can choose to put our emotions to ourselves or learn from criticism and improve our emotional intelligence or let our emotions to control our lives.

Accept full responsibility for your actions. If you feel that you've reacted in an unreasonable and unkind manner, talk to them and say sorry for your actions. The regret and guilt will continue to nag at you and your mind will be taught to stay clear of reactions that can trigger such emotions at some point in the near future. As time passes, you'll be able to control your feelings and behavior under control. Making amends will help the person feel happier and relieve the weight of guilt off your shoulders. You can simply go to the person you are concerned about and admit that you behaved poorly towards them. The majority of the time people are extremely compassionate. They are more likely to be forgiving and forget about grudges. People who are emotionally intelligent know the way they made other people feel, and the effect their actions and words have had on others. Without confronting those who have hurt us and taking the responsibility for our actions we may continue to create destruction in our personal lives as well as in the lives of others.

Learn to manage stress. The feeling that you are overwhelmed is caused by physical stress that life puts on us. To be emotionally smart it is essential to remove any form of stress from your body and mind so that you are able to comprehend your feelings clearly. If someone is overwhelmed by stress, they typically do not have control over the way they behave , and this could cause a variety of negative outcomes. This can lead to increased stress. When we are constantly stressed out it allows stress to make us forget our basic sense and the result is that our extreme feelings and behavior take over us. Two ways to manage stress is either to visit an therapist and get help or record all of your triggers for stress and figure out how to handle the stress triggers efficiently.

How to Handle Emotions

Once we know how to improve your EQ the next step is to discover how to manage your emotions, and to ensure that they don't cause harm.

Here are the steps to be followed in handling your emotions:

Don't react too quickly. Being reactive to your feelings in a moment could mean that you've let your emotions to overtake you out of control. This is a grave error since you're more likely to make a decision that you'll regret. In those brief moments as your body prepares for the emotion you are feeling, take a deep breath , then count up to 10. If your body still has not settled down you can repeat the procedure. This will make sure that you don't make the most costly mistakes of your lifetime. It also provides you with a feeling of satisfaction as you feel confident that you've dealt with your emotions effectively.

Let it go. When you've discovered the depths and darkness of your emotions and succeeded in controlling their impact and feelings, let them go. Express your feelings and emotions to a person close to you through talking to them and trying to make them aware of how you feel. Your emotions are not able to be kept in a closed container. They have to be let out. Discuss your feelings or write about them, and reflect on them frequently. This is the most effective way to manage your emotions.

Allow your family members to forgive you. The main factor that affects your emotional development is generally your friends. It's usually due to what they've said or done in the past, or are doing in present. Perhaps it's because of what you've said or did to them which triggered feelings of jealousy, hatred or even sympathy. If you're angry with anyone, you must learn to forgive them and yourself. The negative emotions you feel can become obstructions that hinder your emotional mental ability. You must remove yourself from this pressures on your emotions.

The primary responsibility for building the ability to deal with emotions and managing emotions rests with you. To enhance your EQ you must learn the strategies that were mentioned above. They can help you assist yourself.

Chapter 4: Start With Honest Self-Appraisal

Can you spot it?

Just in the front you. It is right in front you. Look for it. Because I assure you that it's there! !

"What's there?" you inquire.

I'm happy that you asked. It's you're future, as an Emotionally Intelligent You. And it's a bright future worthy of doing your best for. And that's exactly what this book can help you achieve, discover and develop to become the Emotionally Intelligent You.

Are you up for the challenge? I would like to think that's the case, because there is a door that says Emotional Intelligence, an exciting future filled with strong relationships and rewarding rewards awaits you.Awaits your, that is, if prepared and are willing to complete the work.

The concept of Emotional Intelligence that has gained popularity over the last 20 years, is beyond the catchy that it is at risk of becoming.Many people speak about it, even claiming that they have it, however very few actually know what it actually means.

It's the single most crucial factor in success recognized by man.In fact, research has shown that when it comes to a battle between Intellectual Intelligence IQ and Emotional Intelligence EQ, Emotional Intelligence wins every time. That is to say, people's abilities are more valuable than factual information when it comes to success.If you are forced to decide between a brain or an emotional heart, you should choose the heart.It's ideal to have both. People who are able to understand others are able to go further in life.People who can relate to people , and are knowledgeable in their area, are in the ideal chance of succeeding.

What is Emotional Intelligence? Most sources define it as four categories: Self-awareness Control of oneself, Social-awareness and Relationships management.In simple terms, it is knowing your own self, take control of your own behavior, recognize your needs and those of other people and build positive, mutually beneficial relationships. It's a simple concept, isn't it.But as you'll see at the end of this book getting to be the Emotionally Intelligent You is a complicated multi-faceted procedure that you will not master overnight.But you'll learn it when you've finished this book, which is should you take the time to read it.

Imagine your Emotionally intelligent You as a complex dish (I do not know why, but I like food pictures) A casserole that has 10 ingredients that need to be blended properly and with care to get a great result.Furthermore all the ingredients have to be introduced into the blender in a precise order. That's the arrangement in which this publication is presented.

The objective is to turn you into a well-blended dish that is full of Emotional Intelligence.In your journey, you'll reach an extraordinary level that you thought was not possible.Here's the truly amazing part.Dozens or even thousands (I would like to think so)) could study this book and find the unique Emotionally intelligent you. The book is not an exact cookie cutter.It will, however, utilize a well-established method to produce individualized results.Now let me say a few words about the journey that you're about to embark on.

The best learning comes from personal discovery.In other words, to really learn, you must internalize, personally accept as true and act from a position of commitment and belief.You can mouth words of acceptance.Others might even believe you mean it, but until you are a believer and a practitioner, there will be no commitment.Consequently, this journey to the Emotionally Intelligent You is laced with opportunities for personal discovery I hope you will take advantage of.

For the majority of journeys the point of departure is simple to identify.It's the place you'll be when you decide where to start.In the process of making your way to find the Emotionally Intelligent You, however the point of departure isn't always obvious. The unfortunate thing is that the majority of people do not connect their skills and values to how they earn their money. Consider the thought.It's significance will soon become clear.Here's an hint.Workforce studies have consistently shown that less than 30% of employees on the work workforce in a typical business are truly happy with their work. do.Remember, Emotional Intelligence starts by understanding the self.It seems, therefore, that a small percentage of people embark on the path to becoming the Emotionally intelligent

You.I believe that this is what is what makes you unique.

The most significant purpose for this publication is to give the reader 10 steps for reaching the level of emotional intelligence they were made to be. You were created to be a master in something. Although I'm going to try in this book to help you achieve it, I can only travel alongside you. I'm not able to do it for you.I'll be there with you but I'm not able take you on a journey.

You're about to embark on a thrilling journey that could lead to becoming the most perfect possible version of you. As with all important endeavors working on it, it's difficult, but in this case due to the fact that you'll be scrutinizing yourself, determining your areas of growth and growing.Here are the 10 steps you'll have to follow.

To become what is known as the Emotionally Intelligent You

Find your inner compass. Discover the person you are know the strengths as well as weaknesses. then become the person you're supposed to be and fulfill your life's mission.

Create a powerful goal and vision, and ensure they remain on the forefront of your mind, always.

Enhance your mindset so that you maximize your chances.

Use the force of your emotions to your advantage in positive ways.

Keep your body in good condition and it will last long and long.

Engage in your life and not be an observer. It requires not just a strong dedication but also tremendous energy and determination to make a significant change. If you're not willing to take on the task then there's no reason to be great.

Make sure your internal compass is calibrated for absolute accuracy.Build your life around an unshakeable, personal, developing faith connection with firm values and clear principles , all tempered with a healthy dose of humour.

Spend the majority of your time with those who motivate you and get energy from you.Limit the contact with negative people who can depress and make you feel down.

Learn how to make money and time serve you and not control and manage you

If you think that you know everything you require to know, then you've made the first step to declining. If you don't develop in terms of your intellect, you will fade away. Your brain requires daily stimulation to ensure maximum performance.

Then, consider this one question. "Can do I really afford to leave out one or all of these ten steps towards emotional intelligence that I have listed in the previous paragraph?"

I'm sure you've heard no.If the casserole picture does not inspire you take a look at the ten steps like streets on an actual road map.If you make a mistake in your travels then you're likely to be unable to reach your destination.If you fail to complete one step in your quest for your Emotionally intelligent you, then might fall just short of your final destination.You'll become a better individual certain, but you won't attain the ideal version of you.

You've got work to do and, to begin, let's create a visual representation of where you are currently. To assist you, I've attached the following Emotional Intelligence Measurement tool. Please fill it out as truthfully that you are able to. After that, we'll go over the form.

In fairness, I have to be honest and tell you that this simple exercise is just the first of the many tasks you'll have to complete while working through this book.You might be tempted to skipping some but you shouldn't.

The following table provides an overview of how you are at developing the ten elements of Emotional Intelligence are within your life. Use the rating grid to show how true the statement is to your current life.

#

Life Satisfaction Measures

Rating Grid

1

It is clear who I am and what I am capable of doing and I am living my purpose.

False 1-2-3-4 True

2

My clear and precise vision and goals motivate me, and keep me in the right direction.

False 1-2-3-4 True

3

My outlook is positive, focused on solving problems rather than issues.

False 1-2-3-4 True

4

I can manage my feelings and manage my emotions under control.

False 1-2-3-4 True

5

I take care of my health and body.

False 1-2-3-4 True

6

I am involved in my work, I am important and making a difference.

False 1-2-3-4 True

7

My relationship with God, my values system, and my sense of humor make me feel strong.

False 1-2-3-4 True

8

I am in contact with people that inspire me and also with people who can help me be energized.

False 1-2-3-4 True

9

I am debt-free and am a great money manager.

False 1-2-3-4 True

10

I am an avid learner. I like to experiment, discover and grow.

False 1-2-3-4 True

Score of Total Life Satisfaction

50/50

If you're EQ score is below 36/50, or you've scored one or more measures lower than a 4, it is possible that having a coach help you. I can assist you in that regard. Contact me at 407-703-3730 for help. make the first session. Use this book to get an additional 25% off every session up to five.

How did you fare? If you happen to get an A+, you're doing a fantastic job coloring! You might not require this book. If so I would suggest you take the time to read it, even to have enjoyment, and it's sure to be enjoyable. If your score is low be sure to take the time to read the book. You might you could even call me as I mentioned just a few minutes earlier.

Here, at the beginning, I need to make something clear.I've tried hard to write this book in such a way that individuals from any spiritual or personal background can benefit.I cannot, however, disavow my Christian perspective.It's who I am.It's my major source of strength.Consequently, while I make no attempt to convert you, expect to find a balanced salting of Christian examples.

Let's all learn together. I'll use this and the subsequent three chapters to lay the foundation.Then in chapter 5 we'll begin our adventure with earnest.In the chapter that follows, we've have just completed the first stage of the foundation that is an honest self-appraisal.Next we'll address the problem of differentiation, establishing your self apart from herd.Then we'll look at how you can choose to live your life. And then I'll challenge you to decide what kind of person you'd like to become when you grow old.I would like to do this because aging is something that you will experience regardless of the way you decide to live.Your level of quality of life will be determined by the way you follow these principles.For it's worth it is also what you will experience from now to the present.

Chapter 5: What are Emotions and How Can They Influence Us And Our Performance

The emotions are states of conscious awareness. The average person has only one emotion at a moment. It is usually characterized by an emotional response that is physiological, like excitement. The states of mind are very distinct and individuals have an array of terms that they use to refer to diverse emotions, including fear or jealousy, anger or joy or anger, displeasure, and numerous others. These kinds of states tend to be difficult to trigger and take a long time to go away.

In abstract language emotions are data messages about ourselves and the relationships we have with ourselves. Through recognizing, understanding, and acknowledging the importance of our feelings and emotions to us, we can improve our to perform better. We can aid others e.g. teachers by creating an environment that is conducive to learning and better managing their emotions. will enrich the experiences of students as well as the experiences of their teachers.

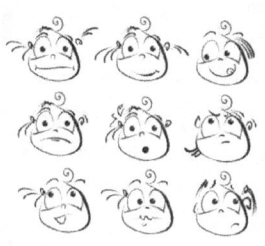

These states should be distinguished from auto-affect that are more frequent than fully-fledged emotions, yet are less often recognized. These are often subtle and perhaps being completely unnoticed. They can be activated rapidly and can appear (and disappear) in just a few seconds

Duty is what makes us perform things in a professional manner However, love is what makes us accomplish them in a beautiful way. -Zig Ziglar of one second. Since they are connected by basic associations and since a person could have many interactions, a person could experience multiple affective responses simultaneously. They might not be so distinct from conscious emotions, and in certain views, affects can be viewed as only one aspect of negative to positive, however recent studies have suggested that affective responses that are not conscious fall into distinct categories that are clearly distinct from conscious emotions. Typically, they trigger an bodily reaction, which includes the arousal process that may take several hours to develop, but it might not be a good source of information for behavioural choices in a rapidly changing or newly developing scenario. The automatic effects are triggered in milliseconds, and are therefore sufficient to contribute to fast responses.

The most commonly used example is that the fear of being afraid causes people to flee. This theory is in line with my the personal experience of both business situations. It also supports compelling evolutionary theories. For instance, an ancestor who was not able to respond to fear could have a tendency to be dangerous.

her genes. In contrast,

The tiger or snake may be killed, and fail to transfer his or her

The ancestors who were fearful would flee these predators and would be able to reproduce. Therefore, today's humans is derived from ancestors with emotions, such as fear.

stimulate other brain regions to trigger activities in other brain regions. The emotion of anger can cause animals and ancestral relatives to fight, which could result in increasing resources or status. Infuriation can trigger an aggressive pursuit of goals. The desire for love can lead people to take part in sexual activity, thus increasing the rate of reproduction. Direct causation suggests that the behavior or at most the initial stages is in some way a part of the state of mind. For example, anger may be a natural trigger for motor movements that are associated with fighting and fighting. Or, the emotional response in the brain may be directly

To think is easy. To act is difficult. To act as one thinks is the most difficult.

The emotion of emotions is what makes people commit destructive, stupid actions at times, but it's not always.

A mood-soothing pill is fantastic and can eliminate the impact of sadness on helping others. It is believed that people who are sad are willing to help other people since they think that doing so others will make them feel better.

The emotional and psychological stress of sadness can cause an increase in consumption of junk food and sweets however, it's only because people believe that the delicious and unhealthy snacks will help them feel better. emotionally distressed. They can also be frozen.

Delaying gratification is a mistake that undermines the wisdom of delaying grat can cause people to

Rewards instead of bigger rewards, delayed ones but not if their moods aren't

Procrastination is a result of sadness However, only if people are able to procrastinate by engaging in pleasant activities that are sure to lift their spirits in addition, (again) only when their moods are believed to be variable.

Emotions and their role

The emotion is a form of information. numerous evidences for the so-called emotion-related modulation in memory. It also helps strengthen the memory traces that are created by emotional effects, it is believed that this information is better remembered than other types of information. emotions seem to concentrate on the most important aspects of an event in a way that they focus in on the most pertinent elements of the incident and therefore learn the important lesson more effectively (as as opposed to learning that takes place without emotion).

The primary purpose and result of unhappiness is that they force people to think over what they have done as well as the things that went wrong, and on what could be different.

Simply having an open mind is not enough; the purpose to open the brain, in the same way of opening the mouth is to close it to something solid.

G. K. Chesterton

The relationship between habit and emotion is also instructive in this case. When individuals perform routine actions that they not feel any emotion as compared to those who engage in actions that aren't habitual.

The power of emotion is usually useful in encouraging learning. In this case, one may conclude from their emotions that they've learned something.

EMOTIONS in BUSINESS

Although some might argue that "emotions when it comes to business" is a misnomer however, the majority of businesses' success is based on motivational goals and the desire to achieve the best. It's true that there's plenty of heart behind the scenes of business and for when businesses are managed by humans that are emotional, there will always be emotions within the business.

It's tempting to think that we're completely free of emotion when it comes to our work-life, but we make decisions using a business mind and not with a bleeding heart. However, our emotions are with us everywhere we travel. For the majority of entrepreneurs they experience both negative and positive emotions can become more acute when making business decisions process , especially during the start-up phase.

It's rare to meet someone who isn't excited about his first client or a successful sale or purchase. The same way, it isn't common to meet someone who isn't afflicted by disappointment after a business experiences an unanticipated setback. It's not a constant business. As with life, it evolves. When these changes are in line with our needs or exceed what we expect, we're thrilled and when they don't our moods take a negative direction.

Beware of negative thoughts that arise from fear. Humans are frightened of many things. We allow fear to influence our rational minds because we're convinced that something will occur, even though there is no evidence to suggest it will.

Mark Hawkins owner of management consulting company in UK experienced experiencing a rollercoaster ride after the credit crunch. "It's an extremely volatile situation," says Mark. In the beginning stages of expanding his business (he is a highly successful manager at a telecommunications company) Mark said, "At the core I believe in myself, but every day I could awake and think"Oh my God What am I doing?' or 'What have you done?' Occasionally you'll be faced with terrifying worries. These aren't rational fears. They're not fears that which you can solve. I believe that's a one aspect of stepping into the unknown, in the quest to build a important business." It's going to require confidence, trust in oneself, self-confidence, confidence and resiliency.

Phil worked for an engineering company. His job was put at risk during recession but he wasn't advised to quit. He took a redundancy offer to establish his own company. He explains the way that many entrepreneurs feel "What typically happens is that you've left something behind to move on to something else and the other thing isn't known. The systems you used to have are familiar. However you may not know the system's requirements and what they are, but you might not even have any system". Doing what you believed was a good business idea is difficult and sometimes unsustainable. If there isn't enough money being received, you're in a negative spiral because you don't have the money to promote for more business. Moreover, you'll need lots of cash to get excellent business contracts. He says that things are more difficult now as you need to consider how you can accomplish these tasks your self."

Beginning a new business is like stepping out to the unknown. Human nature is to be scared of the unknown. This is a typical anxiety for everyone who is entering the in the initial stage of their businesses "What is the consequences if this business is proving to be extremely foolish?" A good number of business owners who are starting out have a basic understanding and background in their area, however they do not have any actual business experience. This is why a lot of research becomes necessary , Phil said - "I needed to look at my own values system and decide which was the most sinful thing, failure or living life in a way that is not my fault? My answer came down to the former. I needed to give it a go."

Nearly every good book or film's plot is unique other than an initial, middle, and an end. We all know that the secret work behind it is the Emotional Structure, the interior landscape. It is the hidden structure that helps to inform the plot that connects viscerally themes of the internal and external world, and directly affects the rhythms and tensions that are the main ideas of the drama. Without the Emotional Structure the beginning, middle, and finally the ending are likely to be an overlapping sequence of the start, middle and finally the conclusion. This is due to the fact that emotion-fluency controls the reader.

10 Quotes to do emotional mastery

1. "Dance like there is no one watching you. Feel as if you've never had a scratch before. Sing like nobody can hear you. Imagine that heaven is here on the earth." Souza

2. "Peace originates from within. Don't look for it without." Buddha said. Buddha

3. "Happiness is not a place you reach rather, it is a method of travel." Marguerite Runbeck

4. "Success does not constitute the sole key to happiness. Happiness is the only way to success. If you are passionate about your work and you are happy, you will be successful." Albert Schweitzer

5. "For every minute that you're angered, you'll forfeit sixty seconds of joy." 5. Ralph Waldo Emerson

6. "Happiness is a conscious decision and not an automatic reaction." • Mildred Barthel

7. "If things make you feel depressed is because you allow you to be affected by them. The results are what we get; our emotions are the result of our emotions. People attach themselves to the outcomes of their lives and to situations that influence their emotions. Each situation has something to learn from and if we're capable of absorbing the lessons that matter and apply them to our lives, we can eventually accomplish the goals we have set out to achieve." -- Celestine Chua

8. "People consider the things they don't want, and attracted to more of the similar." Anonymous

9. "Worrying can be the exact as hitting your head on the wall. It's only good when you put it down." John Powers

10. "Little minds are not worried Big minds have no time to worry." Ralph Waldo Emerson34

Chapter 6: The Eating Regimen

Consume an Diet that is high in nutrients

The nutrients in food aid your body's growth, repair and overall health. The supplements we require include minerals, vitamins, carbs as well as protein and a little fat. Deficiencies in any of these supplements can lead the body to not performing according to their all levels - and could even trigger illness.

Make sure to fill your meal with essential Antioxidants

Free radicals are harmful ingredients that are released in our bodies throughout normal activities, and these free radicals aid in breakage and unnatural maturing. Antioxidants like beta-carotene and vitamin C as well as E combat the negative effects on free radicals. The cell reinforcements are proven to bind these free radicals, and remove their destructive power.

Research has shown brain cells are particularly in danger of being a target for any radical harm. If there's no method to eliminate free radicals in their entirety however, we can limit their devastating impact on our body by taking in foods that are high in cell-based compounds as part of a healthy diet that includes:

Beta carotene sources include apricots and broccoli, carrots, melon peaches, pumpkins sweet potato, spinach, and apricots

Vitamin C sources Blueberries, broccoli grapefruit, kiwi, and oranges peppers, potatoes tomatoes, strawberries

Vitamin E sources sources of vitamin E: butter, nuts, seeds vegetable oils Whole wheat

Take in "Quality" Carbs to get the effect of calming

The relationship with sugars and mood is linked to the brain-set-boosting cerebrum chemical serotonin. Carbs that are longing for could be associated with a decrease in serotonin levels, in spite being that experts do not know whether there's a connection.

In this regard do not ignore all carbs , but instead make smart choices. Reduce your intake of sugary foods and focus on smart carbs (such as entire grains) instead of simple carbs (for instance cakes and sweets) in addition to a wide variety of vegetables and fruits that all aid in the production of in the production of solid carbs as well as fiber.

Eat Protein Rich Foods to Boost Awareness

Protein-rich foods similar to as fish, turkey as well as chickens, are abundant in amino acids, such as the tyrosine. Tyrosine is believed to help maintain levels of the brain chemicals dopamine and as well as epinephrine. This can help you feel more alert and helps you to manage your think. Make sure to include the protein you consume into your diet a few times throughout the day, especially when you are trying to calm your thoughts and increase your energy.

Healthy protein sources beans and peas, Lean cuts of meat and low-fat cheese milk, fish and poultry, soy products yogurt

Consume a Mediterranean Diet

The Mediterranean diet is healthy and balanced diet that adheres to a healthy diet which includes a variety of nuts, fruits, grains, vegetables and fish.

Researchers are unsure if poor supplement intake causes depression and sadness , or if depression can cause people to have food that is not healthy.

Folate is present in Mediterranean food items like nuts, fruits, vegetables and light green veggies. B12 is found in every lean and low fat grass fed animal items like fish and dairy low fat products.

Make sure you have plenty of Vitamin D

A study conducted across the nation found that the likelihood of developing depression is greater among those who are deficient in vitamin D compared to those who have sufficient Vitamin D. In an additional study, researchers of The University of Toronto recognized that people who suffered from depression, particularly those who were occasionally a lot of emotional problems tend to rise the levels of vitamin D in their body increased over the time of the year. Vitamin D receptors are located within the brain. Analysts aren't sure if the amount of vitamin D that is ideal.

Select Selenium Rich Foods

Selenium is an element that can be regarded as a to be a powerful source. There is a connection between lower intakes of selenium and a deterioration in mental state, despite the fact that evidence isn't conclusive on whether supplements could help.

It's possible to consume too much selenium and cause harm. However, this seems unlikely if you're getting it through food rather than supplements. It's no harm to ensure that you're eating food items that help you reach the recommended intake for selenium of 55 micrograms daily for adults.

The good news is that food items high in selenium is a food that we should be eating regardless. These comprise:

Beans and other vegetables

Lean meat (lean hamburger and pork) skinless turkey, skinless chicken)

dairy products that are low-fat

Seeds, nuts or even seeds (such as brazil nuts)

seafood (clams and shellfishes, sardines and crabs, as well as fresh-water fish, salt-water fish and fresh-water fish)

entire grains, pasta cereal, tan rice and many more

Include Omega-3 Fatty Acids into your diet

We are aware that omega-3 unsaturated fatty acids have many health benefits. To date research has revealed that the absence of Omega-3 unsaturated fats can be linked to depression. One study researchers found that groups which consume a tiny amount in omega-3 fats exhibit more frequent instances of depression issues than social groups which consume enough omega-3 fats that are unsaturated.

There are numerous studies that show that those who eat fish on a regular basis as a supply of unsaturated omega-3 fats are more likely to suffer the negative side effects of being discouraged.

Omega-3 fats are known as the essential and primary fats because unlike other substances, they aren't made by the human body. therefore it is vital to incorporate them the form of food.

The richest source of dietary protein comes from fish that are sleek like mackerel, sardines, salmon pilchards and herring crisp, and trout but there is no tinned fish. Studies have shown that the greater the inhabitants of the country consumes, the less is their gloominess.

Increase your intake of B vitamins

People who have lower blood levels of B-vitamin folic acid or excessive blood levels of the homo-cytosine amino acid (a indication that you're not receiving sufficient B6, B12 or the folic harmful) and are more likely to feel demotivated and are more likely to getting a positive result from the higher dosages.

A study that looked at the impact of administering a SSRI using an placebo or the folic corrosive, 60% of patients improved the placebo, yet 90% of them improved with the growth of the folic acid. What is the difference between the folic corrosive itself, which is the shabby vitamin without symptoms, compare with antidepressants?

Folic acid is among seven supplements , the other being B2 and B12, as well as zinc, magnesium, and TMG that assist in regulating homo-cytosine. Insufficient vitamin B3 and B6, folic corrosive magnesium and zinc have been linked to the feeling of discouragement.

A low homo-cytosine level indicates your brain is adept at "ethylating" this is the process through which the cerebrum maintains its research in equalization. It is therefore a positive sign for eating a complete diet and foods that are grown in the ground as well as nuts, vegetables and seeds that are high in these supplements , and also nourishing the multivitamins.

Nourishment Intolerances

If you are suffering from the negative effects of poor concentration, anxiety disorder, insomnia or any other manifestation of tired mental well-being, it's worth looking into whether food intolerances influence your health. Support your serotonin by taking amino acids

Serotonin is created by the mind and body by an amino acid known as tryptophan. Tryptophan is then transformed into an alternative amino corrosive known as 5-Hydroxy Tryptophan (5-HTP) and changes into the neurotransmitter serotonin.

Tryptophan is found in the diet and is found in a variety of proteins-rich foods, like fish, meat beans, eggs and beans. 5-HTP can be found in unusual states of the African Griffon bean, yet it isn't an everyday occurrence in the individuals following a diet.

Insufficient tryptophan could lead to depression; people who advised to eat food that is low in tryptophan quickly became depressed within a matter of hours.

Exercise routinely and exercise by the sun, and also reducing your anxiety level also has an effect on serotonin.

Kava is a root of the kava plant, which is well-known for its calming and relaxing properties. It is usually used as an ingredient in the teas that are relaxing. Some regions in the South Pacific, including Hawaii has used kava to aid in stress relief, temperament increase and various cooling effects.

The results of studies have shown that kava is safe and effective in treating anxiety and depression and anxiety, which can help reduce melancholy-related side effects. But, further research is needed to provide definitive proof.

The Balance Blood Sugar

There is an immediate link between anxiety and the presence of glucose. All starch food can be broken down and converted into glucose, and the cerebrum is fueled by glucose. The more inconsistent your glucose levels, the more erratic your mood. In fact, poor glucose parity is undoubtedly one of the main reasons for depression in those.

Consuming lots of sugar will cause sudden highs and troughs in the measurement of glucose levels in your blood.

The side effects occurring include fatigue or fractiousness. It can also cause tipsiness. an insomnia disorder, excessive sweating (particularly in the evening) Poor focus, lack of concentration, increased thirst, gloom , and shouting spells, digestive problems influence and blurred vision.

Since the mind depends on an the same amount of glucose, it's no surprise that it has been found that sugar is involved in a frenzied behavior, nervousness, depression and in weakness.

A lot of refined sugar and refined carbs (white pasta, bread rice, processed food items) is also linked to melancholia as these meals don't just provide a small amount nutritional value, but they also eat up the capacity to improve B vitamins, transforming each spoon of sugar to vital B vitamins.

Sugar can also divert the flow of an alternative supplement that is included in the your mind set, chrome. This mineral is essential to ensure that your glucose levels remain steady as insulin, which removes glucose from your blood, won't function properly without it. There's information about chromium under.

The best way to ensure that your blood sugar levels stay at a minimum is to follow what is called low Glycerin packed diet. Avoid, in the way you can refined sugars and refined foods, and consuming more whole meals including fruits vegetables, as well as regular meals.

Get more Chromium

The mineral is crucial for keeping your blood sugar steady since insulin, which removes glucose from blood, isn't able to function properly without it. It's easy to see that simply providing the right amount of chromium for those suffering from atypical depression could result in a dramatic improvement.

If you can answer "yes" to at least five of the questions, you are experiencing typical sadness.

Do you crave desserts or other carbs?

Do you tend to gain the weight?

It's possible to say you're tired with no apparent reason?

Do your legs or arms are feeling overwhelmed?

Do you tend to be tired or drowsy for a good portion or all of time?

Do you feel that your feelings are constantly harmed when you are sacked by others?

Did you experience depression prior to the age of 30?

Atypical is a term used to describe the basis that in the majority of the saddened people, they stop their desire, do not consume enough, aren't fit and aren't able to rest. With Atypical, the reverse is mostly authentic.

Atypical depression can affect anywhere between 25-40 percent of those who are discouraged and has a significantly greater proportion of women who are discouraged therefore it's to a large extent common, not uncommon.

A study by Dr. Malcolm the clinical researcher of psychotherapy in the University of North Carolina, suggested that those suffering with "atypical" sadness could benefit from supplementing their chromium levels.

Get enough sun-light

Known in the name of the sunshine vitamin about a third of our vitamin D is found into our skin via the effects of sunlight. Vitamin D deficiency is increasingly becoming an accepted issue across the globe. It could be a cause of moodiness, particularly in the case of feeling uneasy during winter.

The greatest risk of vitamin D deficiencies on the chance you're older (since the capacity to create it within the skin decreases as you the advancing years) and also if you have your skin cleansed (you require 6 times more light than a person who is clean to produce the same amount of vitamin D) and obese (your vitamin D reserves could be hidden within the fat cells) or you tend to avoid the sun, hiding or making use of sunlight. Naturally, you should not risk your skin's health through sunburn.

Chapter 7: The Social Problems that Affect Children

The world is a constantly changing place.There are many challenges facing youngsters today, primarily because of the increasing internationalization and globalization. Many of these issues create anxiety and stress, based on the circumstances, and others have a higher social stigma. This makes it harder for children and parents to receive the needed assistance and support. In order for these children thrive they need constant care of a caring and nurturing caregiver, regardless of whether they are parents or a substitute. It is essential to boost the amount of discussion around these common issues in order to aid the children. The confidence and support caregivers can provides a child will help them develop the confidence and the strength to manage the difficult times with caution. As experienced adults to help our children to ensure that these difficult situations don't have any impact on them negatively on their adult and teenage years.

Making sure they are competent in all social situations is to be thought about and implemented by parents. It is developed as they gain experience and time. It can be achieved through a simple way of teaching vital life skills that will increase their social skills and confidence in any setting they are in. Here are some problems that children face which require understanding and support from experienced adults. The right response to them can equip children with powerful response to any stressful scenario.

Schooling difficulties and schooling

School routines can be challenging and demanding. School days are filled with routines, adjustments and different types of learning, which happen as if they happen in a clockwork fashion. When the school day begins, before class starts, children must be up, washed at breakfast, eat, dress and ready to board their school buses. After school homework and meals are the primary concerns. Children should be equipped with skills for coping to enable them to make the challenges with ease.

Bullying

The negative effects of bullying can affect both the bully and victims, and can have a drastic effect even after the event. The hurt can last until adulthood. It could make a child feel lonely, depressed as well as scared and isolated. Children who are bullied may be vulnerable to various forms of mental disorders that can develop later in their lives. If you suspect that your child has been victimized in bullying, get involved immediately. Give him the tools to deal with the situation efficiently. Instruct him on how to conduct himself in a constructive manner and ensure that you will be there for him.

You may also be required to increase your child's understanding of bullying by helping them to overcome the problem. Help the child understand that it's not their blame, and that the act of bullying is more damaging to the person who is being bullied as opposed to the person who is being bullied. Thank him for doing the right thing and notifying you about it. Make sure he knows that he's not the only one -Many people are bullied at some moment in their lives. Assist your child with the assurance that you'll determine what you can solve the problem together. This will increase confidence levels of your child and provide him the confidence to face the issue. A key part of coping is helping the child to come up with the right phrases to speak to the bully. For example "You shouldn't be doing this in my presence" or "You should keep away from me." Talk to him and encourage him to defend himself without resorting to violence. Help him learn to become a great communication by being assertive and not being aggressive.

CyberBullying

The world of the internet is extremely dangerous to control because it could become a source of rumors and let people speak in ways that they wouldn't normally say in a real-life setting. Cyber bullying is prevalent with young people. It's a type of bullying that happens on the internet using technological devices like mobile phones or computers. It can involve posting, sending or sharing harmful false, harmful or harmful material regarding people. It may also include sharing private information about another person which can cause embarrassment or humiliation. Cyberbullying can be a difficult issue to overcome because the child's personal and social identity is altered through the time spent on the internet. Parents must be very careful about as it could erode the confidence of a child's self-esteem. The anxiety of dealing with the consequences of cyberbullying often erodes satisfaction and happiness and can lead to depression, anxiety and other related stress-related issues. If you suspect that your child is being cyberbullied and you are worried about it, try to offer security and comfort. Share any experiences of bullying that you have had during your childhood may aid your child in feeling less lonely.

Domestic Abuse

Being exposed to domestic violence can increase the likelihood of children developing mental and behavioral issues. Children learn from watching how adults in their lives deal with the stress.

In families that have violent disputes exposes children to emotional outbursts which can affect your child negatively.Children are affected by the incidents that happen within their immediate environment.It exposes children to a variety of behavioral issues and hinders the child's social and emotional development. A child who is concerned about domestic violence may not be able to speak out immediately; the signs begin to emerge when he begins to behave badly at school or at home and crying a lot, or squirting on his mattress. If you're suffering from domestic violence of any kind you should seek out assistance immediately, particularly when the abuse is physical. Find a way to remove your family and yourself from the danger. Find a way to break the destructive patterns and work to reconcile the differences without violence. Children are able to observe the behavior pattern at home and require positive role models; they learn from their example as often or even more than direct instruction.

Parental Divorce

For kids of all ages Certain significant circumstances that alter the family routine or structure, for example, the divorce or separation of a couple at any point can result in an enormous loss and setback. It can be extremely stressful or even depressing. It could test children's capacity to deal with the circumstances. These situations can also affect with the child's psychological and social mental health. To help ease the anxiety of a child when a divorce is going on, talk to assure the child that you're still with him and the divorce will go smoothly. Tell him that, even if you're not living with each other, you'll be there for the person you love. To reduce the effect on the child, be sure that you're on the same page as your ex-spouse about the issue about him. Be sure to adhere to the same set of rules within separate householdsand avoid sabotaging one another's decisions.This isn't easy when there has been a tense incidents, but try to keep a solid and united front whenever you can in the benefit for your kid.

Media influence

Through various media, children are exposed factors that could either enhance or break their self-esteem or general outlook.Studies have proven that exposure to media influences how children see themselves and how they perceive themselves. These perceptions can influence their emotional, physical, and mental well-being. Through media like movies, television and video games youngsters are subjected to unrealistic images of beauty and lifestyle expectations. Because of this, children may develop false opinions about their own appearance. They might think it's inappropriate for their age as well as the general public. In the end, they feel dissatisfied and may engage in reckless behavior to meet the goal but fail to meet the unrealistic expectations they are expected to meet. They get frustrated and depressed when they realize the insanity of their goal and this influences their perception of their own self-worth. The children should also be taught to make the best decisions regarding their entertainment. Films or games that create negative influence should be avoided by their parents. You should be aware of the content your children watch on the television throughout the day. It is crucial to restrict a child's exposure to TV and observe what he is seeing. Additionally, television shows have been found to destroy imagination and imagination in children. There are numerous research studies currently showing that children's abilities who are the ability to think, are affected because they don't have real-time interactions with the world.

Chapter 8: You Can Change Your Mindset

The most important aspect of any strategy that involves changing your mindset is the conviction that the mind is able to be changed. Since so little attention is paid to this crucial element of life,, many people remain with the notion that our minds have been programmed to operate in the manner that they do, and that there is nothing we can do to change that. In many ways, this is a negative thinking by itself. We stare into the mirror and realize that it's empty while enviously admiring those who are gifted with being able to see it as half full. We smile and accept that this is how we were made and must accept what we are. This is a surefire way to spiral downwards, leading to depression.

It is not widely believed that the human mind is immune to alteration. Are you sure that advertising firms would have spent millions of dollars each year pouring their ads into your homes in the event that they didn't believe you could alter your decision? Similar to that politicians invest huge sums of money trying to convince them that their message they're offering is one to believe. All intelligence agencies and governments attempt to change the way that people think. If we weren't able to change our thinking processes, then the education system all over would be nothing.

Minds can be altered , and there's no reason to think that we shouldn't alter our minds to be more positive than we could be. It's only been in recently that people have begun to consider our mental state as either positively or negatively. In the past, the quest for a positive mindset was simply a search for happiness and mankind has been doing it for millennia. The issue of whether happiness and positive thought are one and the exact issue is the subject of debate, however there is certain that the two topics are inextricably linked.

One of the things scientists are finding is that the mind is frequently programmed to bias towards negative. This isn't because we think of things in either a positive or negative manner however, it appears that we cling to the negative longer than we grasp onto the positive. In a study in which half of the control group was informed that a medical procedure was likely to have a seventy percent success rate. The other half was informed that there was a failure rate of 30 percent. The first group saw the procedure in a better light than other group despite the fact they had exactly the same results. The two groups were then revisited and the other viewpoint was emphasized to them. The first group was more skeptical of the process, while the second group remained with the same level of doubt.

There are a myriad of other tests conducted by scientists which have proven that we tend towards negative thoughts, but let's leave the world of science for a moment and return to our personal lives.

When you're in a crowd of colleagues or friends, look around and notice the extent to which conversations are dominated by negative remarks. We all be gifted at identifying negative arguments, as well as a diminished capacity to see the positive. The media provides an illustration of this by the quantity of negative news they provide in contrast to positive news. They don't make this decision without knowing that it's the negative news that is more convincing. We will examine negative thinking processes later on in the book. Now, what's more important is to realize that we aren't machines and can control our mood, attitude and thoughts.

To be more positive, we must begin thinking differently. It is believed who can change their mindset to concentrate more on the positive and less of the negative will begin to see positive results as early as thirty days or less. Like any other skill or acquiring every new skill, there is a bit of effort required along with the determination to stick with it. We'll go over some of the exercises that you can practice to become a better positive thinker in the next book.

What is most important is to begin to believe that the change you need to make from a negative thinking person is possible and entirely yours. Scientists tend to divide people into groups who have a fixed mentality and those who have an open-minded mindset. In research on students, it was discovered that students who were smarter but had established mindsets didn't always perform better than those with lower intelligence , but were more willing to change their habits or putting in more effort to reach their objectives.

It is equally important to believe that maintaining an ever-positive outlook can be beneficial. Keep in mind that the mind naturally retreats back to its old habits and won't put forth any effort unless it is aware that there's a benefit to be realized. I've already discussed certain advantages of medical treatment but there are many more. In general, we like to surround ourselves with people who have more positive thinking. People who are optimistic tend to be less likely to dwell on negative things and are therefore better at resolving issues. They also rebound more effectively from the inevitable tragedies that happen to people in their lives.

We are constantly exposed the world of materialistic consumption and the desire to get more. While this isn't necessarily a bad thing, it can hinder us from seeing the things we already have and makes us focus more on what we don't have. Positive people are much more adept at recognizing the things they should be thankful for than negative people. When they are healthier, more likable and content, those with positive mindsets can be in a position that is more abundant without doing anything else than concentrate on the things they have already.

The positive outlook is not a denial of the reality that life is usually most enjoyable when there are challenges. Even those who are optimistic can't escape this reality however, they seem to bounce back faster and can also learn from the tragedy any lessons that can be taken away. Conversely, those who are negative on the on the other hand, are prone to their thinking processes being overtaken by the negative things which happen within their own lives. We'll soon discuss some suggestions for things you can do to alter your thinking and turn into a positive thinker. How difficult it is will depend on where you're beginning from and the amount of effort you're willing to commit, however, you can alter your way of thinking.

"When you awake each day, you are faced with two options. You can be either positive or negative, an optimist or an optimist or a pessimist. I prefer to be an optimist. It's a matter of perception."

Harvey Mackay.

Chapter 9: Controlling Your Emotions

Denial is the most effective solution for the majority of people in dealing with their emotions. Being open with yourself about what you feel can be difficult, particularly when the emotions are negative. As with an aftermath from a devastating breakup, many people believe that they're happier with no one else. They attempt to convince themselves by trying to feel happy, but they're not able to confront the pain and hurt. The result are broken bridges. In refusing to acknowledge the emotion, people fail to analyze their situation through a rational standpoint and therefore refuse to be able to understand the other party.

A brutal analogy for this particular point is a serious cut to the flesh. It's painful, but manageable. You are aware that a little alcohol can clean it up and eventually lead to healing, but you've decided to not do it because the pain is too much. The wound eventually got infected, and the condition got worse and, before you realize that, the leg will need to be removed.

If you're able to effectively practice Lesson 1, then you've already felt the emotion. How do you handle it? What can you do with alcohol to treat it?

There are four methods to handle emotions. The first is denial, which has been previously discussed and is the most insensitive approach. The other options are competition, avoidance and learning.

Avoidance

As in the previous example The person is aware of the pain of ending the course of a serious relationship. The hole in heart is so large and deep it is clear that all that can temporarily fill it up is alcoholbut not the right sort of alcohol. Other methods of avoiding the feelings is by spending many hours scrolling on Facebook or eating too much or other similar actions.

Another aspect of management is the avoidance of dangers. Because being deeply loved ultimately led to despair, the person chose to decline the chance to chat with that lovely stranger. Even if they had about it, they would have regarded it as nothing but flirting.

Competition

There are some who, as we've mentioned previously is adamant about their feelings, whether it is conscious or not, and wear them as an gold medal around their necks. Instead of viewing it as just a brief period in their lives they eat up this negative emotion and then meld it to their personal identity. When they're out with their friends hearing their stories the people around them would either consider or even say, "I've been through worse."

Instead of controlling your emotions exact opposite was the case. In social situations the first thing these people rather than sympathize with the speaker was to grab the microphone or the spotlight and display their achievements.

Learning

This is the most efficient method that you can find and will significantly improve the quality of every other aspect of your life. In this case, in addition to accepting the emotional state and its origin it is also a way to acknowledge the direction it could provide as well as the learning it given you.

The most emotionally intelligent people view the strong emotions as a signal to take action. But actions can be carried out in two different ways. The first is inward. To illustrate, think of that you are feeling unshakeable frustration with your work. The outside view sees your career as the issue and the only solution is to alter your career path. The inward method however is the more effective and more effective method of action since it alters the perception of the individual or alters the methods that they have employed.

This is the method of emotional management that you should always pursue. To comprehend this approach to management better However, you must to understand and comprehend the emotional three-way triad.

The Emotional Triad

Three factors affect your emotional state, according to psychologists and they're:

Focus

Language

Physiology

Your focus is the way you see the world in a particular moment. When you're at peace or love, the world appears happier and more welcoming because your attention is of the positive aspects of everything. If however, you're feeling down or sad, your attention is on the negative elements of your life. Every daily activities that are handled with ease are entangled with something which makes you feel bad.

The words you choose to use differ based on your mood situation at the moment. Psychologists discovered that depression sufferers have a certain group of words like sad, lonely, miserable and more often than they would normally. Even if the person's mental situation isn't really depression but if there is something negative going on and threatening, they are more likely to say things such as "I am tired," "I can't do this,"" or "This is too hard."

Physiology, as discussed the subject in Lesson 1, is your body language. As you can see from the above picture when a person is feeling that his shoulders are in a slump and his eyes are drooping downwards, and the lips are curved downwards. However when someone is in love the eyes of his partner are round and glowing, his lips are always smiling, despite the absence of any amusing thing and his face is shining and radiant.

This trio will serve as your guideline in taking control of your emotional state. The best part about it is that they're entirely within your control. You don't have to force your family members to call you, or for your partner to tell you "I am so happy for the way you treat me" or "I'm sorry" to feel better, because the power to control emotions lies within you.

The inner action you need to do to manage your emotions is to adjust the balance of the three. In the case of the career discontent example, you may possibly be focused too much on your mistakes. For a better perspective consider your successes.

Exercise 2

This exercise is a continuation of the previous. It's fine to take a break from Exercise 1 for couple of days, but don't immediately follow the exercise with Exercise 2. If you think the first one is already demanding, then you can put it down.

Once you have identified the emotional states in your head at any given moment, and then identifying the root of their impact, consider the possible answers to these questions:

What do I need to know to alter this negative feeling?

What are the things that I think about when I'm in a great mood? Can these thoughts help me to liven up?

What are the projections and words that can alter how I am feeling right today?

Chapter 10: Tips to Find Emotional Control and Tackle Anger Management

If you feel that you're frequently engaged in fights or arguments with others around you It could be the consequence of your anger. Anger is an normal and healthy emotion. However when it is triggered to extreme levels, it may get into a spiral that is out of control. Anger that is uncontrollable can have devastating effects on your life and your mental state as well as your health and your emotional mental health. Understanding the importance of techniques for managing anger and the cause of your anger can help discover ways to control your temper.

Understanding Anger

Anger, in the sense of an emotion is neither good or bad. It's a normal feeling and is a healthy thing to exhibit when you've been treated poorly or cheated. Although anger isn't a problem the way you handle that anger makes a massive distinction. It could not just harm you, but also other people.

Most people believe that when they've got an angry temper they are unable to manage your anger has reached its lowest. We actually are more in control of your anger, than you realize. It is possible to express your feelings freely without harming others. If you are able to do this, you'll feel better and your demands will be fulfilled faster. The art of mastering anger management isn't a simple task however the more you are able to practice more, the greater the chance that it will become much more easy. A good management of anger can affect your goal success, your relationships and the level of happiness with your life.

The importance of anger management

A lot of people believe they have the right to express their anger and that people around them are a bit sensitive. But, anger can be incredibly detrimental to relationships and can hinder your judgement. The emotional outbursts of your life have always been out of the way of achievement and will forever have a negative effects on the way others view your character. If your anger gets into the sky the consequences can be detrimental to your physical well-being.

Being constantly under a lot of tension and stress isn't beneficial for your health. Studies have shown that chronic anger could make you more prone to heart disease and high cholesterol, diabetes an immune system that is weak as well as high blood pressure and insomnia.

If you're angry, you are likely to use up huge quantities of mental energy that could overwhelm your thoughts. This could cause you to find it harder to concentrate, look at the bigger picture, and appreciate your life. Depression, anxiety and various mental disorders are common for those who suffer from frequent anger.

Anger that is out of control can affect how effective your professional career. While creative differences or constructive criticism intense debates are beneficial but constantly yelling at people will likely cause you to be a source of discontent for your coworkers, supervisors and customers further. It could ultimately result in the loss of respect and a bad name will be a result.

Anger can be also extremely dangerous, and can cause scars to people you love and are close to damaging friendships and relationships. If you're constantly angered, very few are likely to trust them.

Tips for Managing Your Anger

Understanding why it's important to control your anger and keep it from spiralling into chaos, you must be aware of the different strategies can assist you in managing your anger. Here are some useful and practical suggestions to help you bring you under control of your temper.

Know the Root of Your Anger

We can't have any events happen without reason. There must be something that causes you to struggle with your anger. The majority of issues that make you angry originate from the things you learned as young. For instance, if you were raised in a family that was violent and you were a child in a violent environment, you may have been taught that anger should serve as a method for expression in order to get everything you want. A high level of stress and traumatizing events may be among the root causes that lead you to be susceptible to anger.

People use anger to hide their feelings of anxiety or vulnerability, embarrassment, guilt, and pain. That means they don't actually feel angered, but instead are able to relate to specific situations that cause them to be angry. These knee-jerk reactions indicate that the anger being displayed is just an excuse to cover up other emotions and demands.

Beware of Triggers of Anger and Warn Signals

Each and every buildup that occurs during an explosion of anger is identified by warning indications. Certain of these warning signs are physical and show up in your body. Anger is the fuel for your fight or flight mechanism that is in your body. the more angry you are the higher the chance that your body will be in overdrive. When you take the time to examine the warning signals of your body, you will be able to begin to control your temper before it goes out of control.

It's incredibly easy to point fingers on others to blame others for problems surrounding you, but forgetting that the primary cause of your anger lies with you and your response to stress-inducing situations. It is not at all to have to do with the actions or actions of other people.

Learn effective methods to cool down

There are many different strategies that can be used to help you calm down and manage your anger. A few of them include:

* Take deep breaths and then slowly breathing out your abdomen.

The exercise routine helps you shed excess energy and help you tackle an issue with a calm mind.

Make use of every sense to help relax.

Massage and stretching the areas that are tense can relax your body and relieve tension.

• Remove yourself from the situation in order to let go of tension and allow you the time you need to rethink your approach.

Find Professional Help

If you've been unable to control your anger by yourself it is recommended that you seek professional assistance. There are various programs, therapies and classes specifically designed for those who suffer from problems with managing anger. A lot of people have similar issues and, together, you can assist each other to over these issues.

Chapter 11: The Practices of Transformational Leaders

As mentioned earlier Transformational leadership encourages the development of capacities, and encourages higher levels of personal dedication to the common goal , and gives the motivation for mission redefinition using clarity of vision.

Consider the leader you are or you currently work with. Are they in a position of leadership that is in which the leader has taken charge of the situation in the manner that communicates an unambiguous vision of the goals of the team expanding and elevating the interests of other members and promoting awareness and appreciation of the purpose and the mission for the entire team?

This is known as transformational leadership.Hence it is possible to deduce on this basis that principles of transformational leadership encompass the following:

A true model for integrity

Transformational leaders are energetic, enthusiastic and driven. They are leaders who focus on making sure that every person in the team achieve their goals and also involve them with the team.

Change is needed

Transformational leaders don't force changes on their the team, they instead create an environment where everyone understands the necessity for change by helping other people to recognize the need to create an "future's" context in which to think and view about the challenges.

Systemic thinking

This entails working and thinking about the multi-faceted needs within the process and how such issues can simultaneously be engaged in parallel progressions. Systemic thinking enhances the consideration of interrelated factors, while developing strategies that embraces efficient networking within the team, in order to achieve more in less time, without undue pressure mounted over any part of the process.

It embraces innovative concepts

Transformational leadership is based on a team that is constantly evolving with new concepts and a willingness to be interdependent with self-reliant thinking. Therefore, strategies, ideas and actions will be developed from a multi-faceted discussions. This will result in not only positive changes within the team but also issues that will unleash the best in everyone.

Collaboration is essential.

Transformational leaders recognize the need for constructive collaboration to develop strategies and concepts to become efficient. In order to develop the right strategies, everyone must cooperate for the benefit of the group, or else there won't be successful outcome. The team must be interdependent to communicate to its members that a variety of ideas is necessary to assist others in becoming successful. To create continuous connections there must be a hierarchy of ideas and a string of inter-personal stimulations.

The components of Transformational leadership

There are four parts of Transformational Leadership that are often known as "the Four I's that comprise Transformational Leadership. These are:

1. Idealized Influence (II)

2. Inspiring Motivation (IM)

3. Intellectual Stimulation (IS)

4. Individualized Consideration (IC)

Idealized Influence (II)

Idealized influence is expressed through the charismatic style and conduct of the leader which encourages others to live by the the core ethics and values. Through being role models and displaying the highest standards of conduct team members can appreciate the extraordinary potential of the leader , as well as the determination that they're directed to achieve higher levels. This acts as an impulsive factor that helps the leader gains trust and credibility on his team members.

Motivational Motivation (IM):

Motivational inspiration comes from the capacity of the leader to inspire people to be committed to the shared vision of the group .to inspire. The leader who is transformational must communicate what the goals of his team and show an adherence to the goals of the team by encouraging confidence and instilling an attitude of unity within the team. To accomplish this, leaders require exceptional communication skills, unrestricted accuracy, constant optimism and energy.

Intellectual Stimulation (IS)

Inspiring intellectual stimulation stimulates innovation and creativity, as well as the putting together of fresh ideas. It thrives when there is a combination of individual effort in the decision-making process and by enhancing team members' in their problem solving abilities. The problem is solved through the encouragement of new ideas and perspectives. Transformational leaders challenge assumptions and provides an entirely new meaning to problems and obstacles through transforming the ways team members approach difficult circumstances.

Individualized Consideration (IC)

Transformational leaders are aware of the person-centered approach to managing the team members individually, because every person is unique. The team members have distinct requirements and have various capacities and potential. Support and coaching should be tailored to their individual requirements and capacities. Particular attention should be paid to their specific needs. Make your follower more effective by assigning tasks. Review and offer improvement suggestions for delegated tasks, and help them work more efficiently. This improves confidence in followers and morale.

By focusing on individual considerations The leader should be able to discern the individual's motivations and provide a variety of individualized opportunities, opportunities for training, and development programs that are tailored to different people or groups of them. This method boosts morale and confidence among employees and allows them to develop and be fulfilled in the various roles they hold.

Chapter 12: Emotional Intelligence

After we've talked about the reasons why the leadership model is changing and is embracing emotions, it's time to discuss about the definition of the term "emotional intelligence. According to the definition, emotional intelligence refers to " the capacity to recognize and manage your own emotions as well as of others, and even of groups." In essence, as leaders, you'll be utilizing the power of your own emotions as well as your employees' emotions to create a positive and effective environment. The ability to be emotionally intelligent is to control your own emotions and manage your mental state, as in addition to being able to discern and influence the state of mind that your staff members. This book will provide you with different methods that will enable you to increase your emotional intelligence and become an emotional leader.

Why emotional intelligence is important

They are extremely powerful, and if you're able to communicate on an emotional level between your workers, you'll be able to easily motivate and motivating your employees. Think about the different personalities who have the ability to inspire. They all have one thing that they all share. They are all extremely emotional. They range from Tony Robbins to the best football coaches, they're all very emotional. If you're hoping to become a successful leader and inspire your followers, you must draw on and make use of the potential that your feelings have. Becoming in control of your emotions, and staying at peace in the face of uncertainty and fear is the hallmark of excellent leaders. It is an indication of a good degree of intelligence. Controlling your emotions in any circumstance will motivate your team members and create an atmosphere that is based on confidence. Compare this to a leader who is struggling to manage their emotions, which can result in a stress-filled environment and tension. People with an emotional intelligence that is high will also be be able to discern and comprehend the feelings that their staff members. The issues will be identified quicker and a greater understanding of the needs of the employees will enable rapid solution-finding. Additionally, you will be able to inspire and motivate your employees, resulting in a rise in productivity. Being emotionally connected to your staff will enable both of you to be united in their goals and work towards the same objectives. The ability to communicate emotionally will allow you to bring your employees together and help take your business up a notch.

Emotional Intelligence as well as the Hiring Process

The last time we spoke, companies are only getting to know the value of emotion intelligence. Many millions of dollars is spent every year on training and hiring new leaders and managers just to see some achieve success. The companies have invested a huge quantity of funds and time to discover why certain managers are successful while others fail. They have concluded that emotions are the key factor that determines the effectiveness of managers. Employers will screen for emotional intelligence in job interviews, and asking you specific questions concerning your experience with your coworkers, rather than inquiries based on intelligence. They'll also ask questions more personal to you that are specifically designed to provoke emotion. Employers are seeking people with an excellent emotional intelligence score and who are willing to pay premiums for the ability to be a leader.

The Fall of Old Leaders

There are many characteristics that define the old managerial style which companies are trying to replace. To analyze the shortcomings of leaders as well as employees, it is necessary to begin at the very beginning in the process of hiring. The traditional way of hiring employees are selected by their academic and intellectual expertise. Students with the highest grades would be offered the best jobs, and their ability to be emotionally intelligent or to collaborate together was never in doubt. This method of hiring the brightest and most talented students resulted in great results when employees were employed in entry-level positions. They could use their expertise for a specific job and were typically told to keep their heads down and to work as hard as they could. After a couple of years, a manager job would become available and the employee would become qualified for a promotion. This is where the previous system starts to unravel. Our employee has the challenge of communicating with people in real time this is a task he not properly prepared for in college or in his first job. Our employee was promoted from a job of processing numbers to dealing with and solving emotional issues.

Our new boss will enforce policies and rules that reflect his management style, without taking into consideration the needs or emotions for his workers. The office's new motto is "his ways or highways." This results in lower morale in the office and lower productivity. Managers become annoyed when quarterly reports do not meet goals. Instead of calling with your office for help, the manager concludes that the issue is due to a poor working habits. New rules and longer working hours are implemented , and they begin to create a hostile work environment. Managers become frustrated with the progress made and loses control of his emotions. When this happens the manager is merely counting the days until he's replaced. It's because it was never his error in the first instance. He was never taught about emotional intelligence or instructed to study the psychology behind emotional intelligence. The only time he was familiar with emotional intelligence came from his interactions with acquaintances, which is different than managing and leading employees.

Creating An Environment For Success

We have already given an illustration of how the current system has failed managers today. we'll give some examples of the characteristics employers are seeking in their new managers and leaders. We'll begin by introducing the hiring process , similar to like the one above. The difference between our firm and that which did not succeed is how they screen applicants in interviews. Our company is cutting the list of candidates they are considering hiring by grading and abilities however instead of securing the best metric-based candidate, they screen to determine if they have emotional intelligence. Instead of choosing the person with the highest tests and memory for photos the company decided to hire one who demonstrated ability to recognize emotional intelligence. The new employee is put in a position of entry-level where they utilize the abilities they learned in the college classroom. They are required to take part in classes and workshops that help develop emotional intelligence. They're often assigned to mentors across the office. After a few years, time, our employee gets promoted to a managerial job. They're able to lead and manage with emotional intelligence as they've been trained and taught in the development of these skills over the last few years. In lieu of being overwhelmed they're at ease with their job and the ability to manage. This is how businesses would like their hiring process and management to go. If you recognize the value of your emotional intelligence and strive to develop your abilities to improve it, you will climb in the ladder of corporate success at quicker rate and also be ready when it's time to manage and lead.

The changing landscape of emotional Intelligence

Let's be clear about the basics before we start instructing you on how to increase your skills in emotional intelligence. A focus on just emotional intelligence won't result in a job or even the management role. It is also necessary to possess the ability to think critically and have a solid understanding of business. You may have exceptional emotional intelligence , however you won't be able to get an interview with the equivalent of a 2.0 GPA. This is the same for management. You won't be given a leadership job if you've got an insufficient understanding of your industry and a bad attitude to work. You must be balanced in your search for and understanding of specific skills. There are some organizations who are slow to embrace and appreciate the significance of emotional intelligence. Although these companies might not be able to recognize your abilities, having an emotional intelligence skills will help you in many ways both in your personal and professional life. Don't get dismayed or be afraid to use emotional intelligence even in case your employer isn't looking for this particular skill. This is a skill that will benefit you in virtually everything you undertake.

Chapter 13: What happens If We Do Not Make Time for Recovery?

Since most of us are juggling many different areas of our lives within the same day it's hard not to be overwhelmed in these times. According to a recent study, 87% of the managers who were questioned stated that their phone was in use outside of normal working time and on the holidays, causing them the impression that they are not able to shut off.

Work is regarded as the primary contributor to stress levels rising It's not surprising that we all find ourselves overwhelmed from time the time. This is why we need to remember the phrase, 'from time the moment'. This is because the majority of us can take a break and relax in our day. What happens when you're feeling constant tension for a prolonged period of time, and the recovery process isn't possible?

When your body is subject to constant stress for a long period of time it is likely that the Amygdala is always detecting dangers and directing the body's responses. It shuts down the rational frontal lobes and triggering the more popularly known as an 'amygdala hijack'.

If you don't get the proper recovery, your mind as well as body won't have the time to recover for the day ahead which will leave you with the exact same feeling like the day before.

Consider a different approach to your water balloon.

The amygdala keeps firing, pins are making small holes inside the balloon, and the water levels are slowly going downwards. In the absence of a recovery period for blood cells to fill in these holes, and allow levels of water to rise up, the capacity to manage stress is deteriorating and starts to affect other brain regions.

The Hippocampus is the brain responsible for motivation, memory and controlling emotions. It is among the areas that suffers from excessive stress. Have you ever felt immersed in stress to the point that you want to vent, and get angry in a way that is more severe than you planned? This is just one of the effects we're discussing here.

Research has shown that studies have shown that the Hippocampus actually begins to shrink within the brain of those experiencing high stress. This is the reason why people who are going through extremely emotional or traumatizing events are experiencing memories fading and emotional instability. This is quite scary, isn't is?

The good news is the fact that it doesn't mean we need to let our hippocampus go to fend for itself in the dark...we can take action about it.

By focusing on stress management and simple methods like mindfulness, we are able to reverse the consequences. Our minds are flexible substances and we are able to alter the neural pathways within our brains by implementing and practicing various thoughts.

In reality, we are able to train it so well that we are able to alter the shape and size of certain brain regions. This is very special.

Chapter 14: What is Emotional Intelligence?

Emotional intelligence is the ability to identify, assess and manage one's emotions. It's actually the emotional component of the brain.

Emotional intelligence, also known as EQ was a newly established behavioral representation that gained the level of distinction in 1995. The first theory of emotional intelligence was created during the 70s and 80s. It is increasingly relevant for executive development and the rising generation.

Through the use of emotional intelligence, new strategies were devised to better understand and analyze the behaviour of individuals. This is the case for their attitudes, management styles, and interpersonal abilities. Emotional intelligence can be utilized as an important element in the preparation of human resources as well as job profile, management development and customer interactions as well as other areas. Emotional intelligence is strongly associated with spirituality and love which bring compassion and understanding to the workplace.

For some, EQ is more important than IQ in the pursuit of a successful career and in life. It is essential to recognize signals from other people in order to be able to react appropriately. It is essential to develop emotional intelligence so that one can recognize how to comprehend, communicate and interact with others.

The concept of emotional intelligence could also be defined as the ability of a person to communicate with others by understanding what drives them and how to interact with them in a respectful manner. Simply put it's the process of recognizing and understanding how a person responds in a given situation.

There are four aspects of EQ that is to say;

The first step in being able be able to comprehend your feelings is to to discern them clearly. This is a matter of understanding the body language and facial expressions.

Thinking with Emotions - the second step involves the utilization of emotions in order to improve decision-making and cognitive stimulation. Your emotions can help you focus on the things you observe and then act in response.

Understanding emotions - Your emotions have a variety of implications. Any action that someone observes in you is associated with a particular sensation you feel and in turn.

Controlling Emotions - This is the most important aspect that makes up emotional intelligence. Refusing to your emotions, reacting appropriately and responding to emotional reactions of people with respect are all component of emotional management.

Your EQ is determined by the following methods;

Self-reporting an test designed to evaluate one's skills that include stress tolerance and attentiveness, as well as crisis-solving and happiness.

A test based on ability that requires the student to perform tasks designed to assess their ability to discern, recognize and appreciate, as well as make use of their emotions.

A screening test that is designed to determine one's pessimism as well as optimism.

An inventory of emotional competence that asks people to evaluate the ability of a person on a variety of emotional skills.

How can you use Your EQ to your Workplace and in your Relationship?

Emotional Intelligence IN THE WORKPLACE

The ability to communicate emotionally is crucial when working. Being able understand your colleagues in a caring manner will help you build a stronger work relationship and, consequently leading to more harmony in the workplace and more productive work.

Utilizing your EQ at work can help you react effectively in stressful situations colleagues or even the workplace itself. This can prevent arguments and even reduce the chance of making a decision without proper thought. It also helps you trust that you are able to handle any task at any time and successfully complete it.

Being successful as a businessperson in this current fast-paced business world requires more than providing a high-quality product or service to offer. It is of paramount importance to to manage your business with an elevated emotional intelligence to manage clients and employees more effectively. Here are a few steps you can follow to increase emotional intelligence in your business:

With clients

Always show up on time. Always arrive early for scheduled meetings. If you are a bit late, be prepared to apologize. Make sure you are punctual with your delivery. If you're unable to meet a deadline, attempt to make up with discounts.

Always arrive prepared and well-equipped for meetings with clients. This will demonstrate to your customer that you're serious about business.

Always be warm in your words, actions and tone. Let your customers know that they are not only in the business aspect but as a person than anything else.

Be compassionate when working with your clients, and take into account their emotions when deciding on certain issues.

Value principles are more important than profit. Be prepared to compromise and to be flexible in accommodating the needs of your customers.

Be a leader with a great spirit of humor. It's best when you carry the image of someone who is committed to handling his clients, but not overly stern at the same time. It's not a bad idea to laugh or make some jokes at least once in a while.

WITH EMPLOYEES

Be aware of your expectations. Your employees must clearly be aware of what you want from them, so that they are capable of meeting your expectations more effectively.

Do not be afraid to praise your employee for their work. It's always nice to know that your boss is pleased with the work you've done.

Treat employees with respect. Any criticism or warnings regarding performance that falls short of expectations must be handled with a quiet tone. Do not call attention to them within the ears of their fellow employees.

Inform your employees that you are concerned about their well-being and feelings. This will motivate employees to do their best work.

Emotional Intelligence in Your Relationship

One of the key elements to ensure a relationship lasts is a good level of communication. In order to attain this emotional intelligence is important. It is said that to better communicate with others it is vital to know what's going on inside their minds and how they respond to specific situations. The success of a harmonious relationship depends on your ability to communicate and understand effectively with one another.

If a relationship is in its beginnings it is common for both parties to showcase their best sides. Everything appears to be right in the eyes of each other because the negative side is being kept hidden. As time passes the positive traits begin to disappear and the negative traits begin to show up. What is the reason for this? The relationship's emotional intelligence has fell away. Both parties have stopped being in a position to recognize and comprehend the other's needs and feelings.

A successful and satisfying relationship requires the use of a set of skills that are totally distinct. It is not a gift that comes to people from birth, but is learned through experience. Sometimes, because of the emotional baggage of an individual that he is not in a position to apply these abilities in his relationship. If you are looking to dig into the deeper layers of your relationship, it is recommended to get rid of any emotional baggage prior to embarking on the relationship.Here are some guidelines to create a successful relationship through emotional intelligence

Always follow the golden rule when it comes to your relationship. If, for instance, there's a heated debate and you are tempted to fight your way back the best you can, do not. Whyis that? Everyone is prone to speak out in a negative way in the midst of anger and then regret it later. Be vocal when the rage is finally gone and stop your emotions from influencing your actions and words. Both of you will be able to solve the problem in this manner.

Be sure to show them your love. You wouldn't want to remain in an intimate relationship that is filled with affection and love, wouldn't you? Be a kind, caring and loving partner. This will create more positive energy to your relationship.

Be sensitive to your partner's moods - In order to enjoy a pleasant relationship, both of you should be aware of what's happening within your relationship emotionally. Be aware of body language; look for signs that something is troubling the person or if they are satisfied with things.

Controlling non-verbal messages It is an effective way to keep the relationship on a positive level. Eye contact, facial expressions or a gentle pat on the shoulder or cheeks is a great way to let them know that you are understanding and caring. It lets the person you are with feel that you're there without needing to express it.

Don't rely on your heart when making decisions concerning the relationship. Although it is claimed that your heart's the one responsible for the emotional aspects of a relationship, don't think that you can't use the power of the brain. If things go wrong and you're feeling very angry you are likely that you'll end up coming to bad choices that you'll regret afterward. Do not let stress and emotional turmoil make you the wrong partner.

Be quiet for a few minutes and then just take a moment to listen. It's not always necessary to discuss things. Sometimes, your partner requires someone to listen. Someone who will be able to understand his hopes and failings.

Support from your family or friends If you've been in an argument with your partner, it's recommended to talk about the issue with a close and trusted friend or family member. They may be able to suggest the solution or idea that you may not have thought of.

Are you interested in knowing how you are doing in the area of emotional intelligence in your partner? You can answer these questions:

While listening to what your companion is saying, are more attentive or do you drift off quickly?

If there is no sound during the discussion, are you content?

In making an important choice, are you the kind of person who trusts your instincts?

When you are mediating through turbulent times, do you remain in a position to make use of humor?

If you are in a stressful circumstance can you be calm?

Do you handle the nuances and differences in a fair manner?

If you're able to answer the questions above then you're an emotionally intelligent spouse. If the answers are generally not yes, you should work on improving your emotional intelligence during your time together.

Chapter 15: The Primary Emotions of Plutchik

Let's take a look at what exactly we need to be aware of about each emotion and how each affects an individual in different situations and how we can benefit from it by having a fundamental but most valuable "Emotional Triggers Grid" to look over, before getting into marketing campaigns. These emotions are linked regardless of the business sector.

While there are many theories of emotions proposed by various researchers at different periods The most popular model originates one from Plutchik. The Wheel of Emotions is one of the theories widely used by researchers of today and psychologists. It reveals the connection between the emotions common to humans. We have simplified the list of emotions by focusing only the primary emotions that are further divided into Negative and Positive emotions.These feelings, both positive and negative are the two poles of earth, which are in opposition each other, and cannot exist without one another also.

Positive Emotions

Positive emotions are the ones that inspire us to take action towards the things we desire to be experiencing. That is you can declare an effort or a desire to include. For instance, engaging more with other people, expressing joy in the process of making things better, etc. Positive emotions are fuelled by a deep-seated desire for joy and unity.

Positive emotions, for example, are: Joy, Love and Trust. They also include anticipation, anticipation, and trust.

Joy: To feel happy with (or having fun with) something or an thing or

Surprising: Being delighted with something that happened unexpectedly or was completely unexpected and unpredictably

Faith: To believe in one's capabilities or one's self to accomplish or act in the right way

Anticipation: To anxiously anticipate an exciting event anticipated to occur

Negative Emotions

Negative emotions can be those which drive us to get rid of the things we don't desire. They signal an effort or desire to eliminate.

Negative emotions, for instance, include: Anger, Fear Sadness, Fear, Anger

Anger: A state of mind of displeasure that can vary in intensity, ranging from mild irritation to extreme anger and fury

Fear: A negative emotion created by the fear that something or someone is risky, likely to cause pain or threat.

Sadness: A feeling of sadness that is triggered by discontent, loss of hope, despair, and grief.

Disgust: Feeling of anger or profound disapproval triggered by something that is unpleasant or offensive.

What do Psychologists and researchers think about emotions?

Emotions are the most important ingredient for motivation. They drive people to take action. Here are some additional comments that demonstrate the importance of emotions:

A famous Neuroscientist Antonio Damasio states: In an ever-changing world emotions are viewed as shortcuts that allow us to make decisions. according to Dr Marcel Zeelenberg says 'feeling is to be used for action'.

"Although beliefs can guide our decisions, they are not enough to trigger actions. Emotions are the best way to making a person who thinks to acting." (Frijda, N.H., Manstead, S.R. and Bem, S. (2000). The impact of emotions on beliefs. in N.H.

Frijda, A.S.R Manstead as well as S. Bem (Ed.) Beliefs and emotions

As Lazarus is a famous psychologist studying emotion, said "Before emotion takes place individuals make an automatic, sometimes unconscious evaluation of what's taking place and what it could be affecting them or the people they take care of. In this way emotion is no longer rational, but an essential element of our survival.'

Okay, let's go into the following chapter and learn more about the Triggers that affect our emotions.

Chapter 16: The Tools to Control Your Emotions

Being able to keep your emotions in check is more than just the ability to control your emotions requires more than a willing heart. Being able to see a situation through the eyes of someone else and enhancing self-management skills and self-awareness are instruments that you can use in the quest to control your emotions.

The Other Side

If you're ever trying to know what kind of person you are, and the way you conduct yourself, talk to your friends and family members. It's easy to justify what you do, that it appears that every action you take is flawless. If you were to take a honest examination of yourself, you'd likely conclude that it is not just is not the case for you, but also that it is not achievable for everyone.

Discuss with your coworkers, bosses or your friends about the way they perceive your character. If someone saysthat "When everything goes your way, you're an excellent person If things don't work out as you would like and you get angry, you've got an explosive temper' do not get angry and don't immediately assume it's not true. Knowing this information is an important tool that will allow you to manage your emotions. Your emotions and the way in which you communicate them are yours to control. If you don't like it, fix it.

Self-Management and Self-Awareness

Self-management can be difficult to control when self-awareness leads to an self-centered and arrogant outcome. The strength of self-management as well as self-awareness is at the intersection of these two. Knowing what you're about and the position you fill as well as the authority you hold are all crucial but if they interfere with your ability to be accountable and consistent that could lead to an unsatisfactory outcome. In the same way when one isn't aware of who they are and their significance, this can affect their ability to remain reliable and accountable. Individuals who know their ways for dealing with conflict and comprehend the significance of their ways of conducting things aren't likely to cause more problems than those who aren't conscious of their own actions.

Don't give up and keep trying.

It is a necessary aspect of dealing with people in the world of business as well as in personal relationships. The ideal scenario is that everyone would agree with everything you have to say, however that is not likely. If you're not in a world that doesn't value diplomacy it is an ability that will provide plenty of opportunities for you to learn it.

This could be more challenging when you're in a position that has lesser influence. It is possible that you will be required to compromise at a higher extent or even follow the advice of your superiors without considering your own personal beliefs or feelings. In any case, understanding how to be able to hold your beliefs and accept the opinions of others and not creating tension within the relationships is essential for your success at workplace.

Practical Illustration

Henry was at his desk was trying to write an article while his manager, Todd, interrupted him. Todd advised Henry his boss that he's too slow in the turnaround time. Todd was tempted to get his anger out and tell Henry that he had more work to do this week than he had in the past but he was aware that excuses will result in nothing. He tried to realize that his boss is getting the same treatment as his boss regarding his work that he was doing, and he tried to inform his boss that he'd attempt to perform his work quicker and more consistently. Todd acknowledged his gratitude and walked off, turning an argument that could've been a heated argument turn into nothing.

Chapter 17: The Building Blocks of Emotional Intelligence

In the previous chapter we talked about how important it is to be aware of yourself we'll now discuss ways to implement it, along with the other steps to improving your emotional intelligence. Every process is a process that includes emotional intelligence. exception.

Self-Awareness

Controlling how much stress you feel is the beginning of building emotional intelligence. Science behind the concept of attachment suggests that the current environment you live in may reflect your experiences as in your early years. Your ability to manage your emotions, including fear, sadness, anger and joy is contingent on the quality and consistency of your emotional environment. When you were a child If your primary caregiver appreciated and respected your feelings, then it's likely that your feelings will be an asset to you throughout your adulthood. If your experiences with emotions when you were a child were scary or confusing, or even difficult, it's possible you've tried to separate yourself from what you're actually experiencing.

But, being able to feel your emotionsand to keep an unwavering connection with your feelings is the most important factor to understand how emotions impact your behavior and thoughts.

Let's examine the situations that are facts to you in your own life. If these scenarios aren't for you then perhaps your senses may be "turned off. To develop the emotional intelligence of your children, you need to first get back in touch with your inner emotions, be able to accept your feelings, and then become comfortable with them.

Do you experience different emotions as your surroundings shift from one moment to the next? Do you feel that your emotions are constantly changing?

Do you feel your emotions are expressed by physical sensations that you feel in your stomach, throat or the chest?

Do you experience one emotion or sensation like joy, sadness, anger or even fear? These emotions is evident in your calm facial expressions?

Do your feelings influence the choices you make? Do you pay attention to the feelings you feel?

A way to become more aware of your feelings and how they impact your life is to practice mindfulness. Mindfulness is the act of paying attention to the present moment without judgment. Many religions offer some kind of prayer or meditation method that is similar to meditation, however it is not a religious practice. For those who want to begin the practice of mindfulness to be more in tune with your feelings, you should adhere to these guidelines.

For a few minutes, try to pay attention to your breathing. Do not control it, just concentrate on the breath.

Be aware of the way you're feeling. Are you feeling positive unhappy, miserable and sad, happy or uncomfortable?

Which word is best to describe the emotion you're experiencing?

Pay attention to that emotional intensity, the quality of your respiration, the posture of your and whatever else you're experiencing within your body.

Pay attention to the thoughts and opinions that you're experiencing. It is possible to hold on to positive feelings while letting go negative thoughts however, you must be aware of your thoughts, and then consider them as either positive or negative.

If any other feelings arise take note of the feeling that is arising in your mind. Recall the same way you described in steps 2 and 3.

When you're done then take some time to consider the ways you might hold on to or deny certain emotions.

Self-Management

To be able to make use of the power of your emotions, you must to be able to utilize your emotions to make sound choices about your actions. If you're stressed it is possible to lose control over your emotions, as well as the ability to act in a manner that is appropriate and with a sense of prudence.

Remember a time that you felt overwhelmed by anxiety. Did you find it easy to make a rational choice and be clear on your thoughts? Most likely it wasn't. If you were under stress the ability to think clearly and rationally was diminished.

Emotions are a significant aspect of your life that can tell you about yourself as well as those who surround you. However, when you're under stress that takes you away from your comfortable zone it is possible to become overwhelmed and lose the sense of who you are. When you're able control stress and remain present emotionally, you are able to accept information that may be negative but you retain your control. It is possible to make choices that allow you to manage your impulsive behavior and emotions and manage your emotions in a healthy way and take initiative, adjust to the changing environment, and keep your commitments.

One method to instantly lower tension levels instantly is to breath in through your nose slowly, not closing your mouth in order to breathe out. Take a moment to feel the air filling up your lungs and let it go slowly and gently. This is a great way to give yourself some time to contemplate the things you'll think or say before you speak or act.

Social Awareness

The third element of emotional intelligence is to be aware of the emotions of others. Social awareness helps you identify and identify the non-verbal signals others are using in order to convey their feelings. These signals inform you of what someone's feeling, what their emotions are in a given moment and what is most important to them. When a group of individuals give a similar non-verbal cue, you're able recognize the importance of interactions and better read them. In the end, you're relaxed and friendly.

Another area in which mindfulness can be a huge help. In order to increase your social awareness, you need to acknowledge the significance of mindfulness when it comes to social interactions. It's difficult to discern subtle, nonverbal signals that you're always contemplating yourself, contemplating other things, or completely lost in your thoughts. Social awareness demands that you be present at the present moment. Although many people are happy to be multitasking however, it means that they're not noticing the subtle emotional signals being displayed by others which will allow you to understand the person you are talking to more.

Take your thoughts off the table and concentrate on the conversation that's taking place. You're more likely to accomplish your social goals by doing this.

Pay attention to the patterns of other's emotional reactions Be aware of your own.

Pay attention to the other person Be aware that it's not degrading your own self-awareness. When you devote effort and time in paying attention to other people you gain understanding of your emotional state as well as your thoughts and values. For instance, if are irritated by someone else's opinions, you've learned something about yourself.

The Relationship Awareness

The last building block is a sense of relationship. Making friends with peers or spouse and family members, friends and strangers starts with an awareness of your emotions and the ability to detect and understand what other people are going through. Once you've developed an awareness of emotions you will be able to build additional social and emotional abilities that will improve your relationships.

There are 3 ways that you are able to become more aware of your emotions when it comes to relationships.

1. Be aware of the ways you communicate non-verbally.

It's impossible to not be communicating non-verbal signals to people in your vicinity about the way you're feeling and thinking. The various muscles in your face, specifically those around your eyes, mouth the nose, forehead, and mouth allow you to communicate your feelings and also read the intentions of others. The emotional portion of your brain is constantly operating, and even if prefer to ignore its signals and others don't. Understanding the nonverbal signals you communicate to others around can play a crucial part in improving the quality of your relationships.

2. Use laughter to ease stress.

Humor and laughter are both natural stress alleviators. They ease your stress and can ease the burden while keeping things in the right perspective. Laughter can help bring your nervous system to an equilibrium, decreasing your stresslevels, relaxing you down, sharpening your wits and allowing you to be more compassionate towards yourself and others.

#3 See the conflict as an opportunity for you to build relationships with the person you are with.

Conflicts and arguments are part of every relationship. There is no way for two people to share the same requirements, expectations, or opinions on a daily basis. But, this doesn't have to be a negative thing. The ability to resolve conflicts in a positive way can strengthen the bond between two individuals. When conflict is not viewed as a threat or punishment and can foster confidence, independence and security within the relationship.

Once you've mastered the fundamental elements that make up emotion intelligence, we can get to discover which emotions you're feeling and also how to discern the emotional signals of others.

Chapter 18: What makes an emotionally strong and Intelligent Person?

It's hard to determine emotional intelligence. While certain psychological tests may yield results, they're costly and most people never attempt these tests. The ability to express emotions is "the quality" everyone has. Based on the level of it is, an individual can manage their behaviour as well as make personal choices and be a part of society.

Researchers have spent decades looking at the data of more than one million people who had their EQ assessed. The tests they took were used to determine the level to which an EQ level could go.

Before you conduct a psychological test with a professional to determine the level of your psychological intelligence look at the following characteristics that emotionally intelligent individuals have in common.

1. People who have a high EQ accept change. The most terrifying thing for most people is the idea of change. We are all aware that the only constant thing that is constant is change, we still worry and fear that change is inevitable. The funny thing is that we all imagine the worst outcomes of any possible change in their lives. For instance, if you leave a job you don't like and let your brain imagine the worst scenario that could happen (in which you can't find a better job , or your business plan is unsuccessful and you end up losing all your money and are forced to go to the streets) You avoid the joy of a change. Instead of elevating your energy by imagining the best scenario and keeping yourself in a cheerful mood (and by focusing your attention on creating positive emotions) instead, you decide to stay scared and stay in a negative mood.

The most emotionally intelligent people aren't afraid of change. They accept it and view it as something exciting. It's always changing which is why we can easily shift between two realities without worrying that things will be bad. likely to occur along the way.

2.People who have a high EQ don't fear feeling discomfort - As we've seen in previous chapters, the majority of people believe that emotions are negative and should avoid them. People look for places to hide away from emotions for example, relationships and money drug use and power, fame and other things. A person who is emotionally strong doesn't require areas to hide. Someone who is emotionally strong is one who allows their feelings to take place. If you stop denying or ignoring your feelings your control is lost. Instead of trying to escape your feelings of fear, anger or anxiety or any other emotion you're feeling ensure that you're not scared from feeling that emotion. The emotions you feel won't harm you by letting them flow through your body.

3.People who have high EQ want respect and not approval or attention. Check out your social media accounts and look around at all the users seeking approval and attention through just one "like". It's truly sad to see how low human beings have fallen; the need to be noticed isn't atypical however, it can cause a lot of unhappiness as people seek to achieve social dominance by continually attracting attention. It's true that attention does not have to come as simple as a "like" or a photo. It could come in the form of someone who's constantly annoyed by absurd things, as they are the sole way they can get attention from their family or spouse. Attractiveness can manifest in the form of inciting excessive drama, lying or even gossiping. A person who is emotionally intelligent will seek to earn recognition instead of being noticed since they realize that they don't need to be the center of attention to feel comfortable.

4.People who have a good EQ can recognize their individual needs as well as their fellow human beings' needs. They don't think that another person's feelings and desires are less important in comparison to their own. In addition someone with EQ won't be able to deny their own needs due to the opinions of others. opinions.Adults who were taught to believe that the needs of their parents were more important than their own lived lives that put the needs of everyone else ahead of their own. This isn't a sign of emotional intelligence; more of a method to allow people to walk over you and take advantage of your trustworthiness.

5.People who have high EQ consider failure and criticism as learning experiences, not evidence that they're not worthy. A person who has an EQ of high EQ doesn't look for external validation for their own worth, nor do they consider criticism to be an personal offense. Highly emotional intelligent people consider criticism, and even failing as tools that will assist them in gaining and growing. People who have poor EQ will cry and get furious at criticism, no matter if it's related to their job, lifestyle or any other part that they live in. They'll say that people dislike their style and envy them, which is often not the case.

6.People with a high EQ will not try to control their feelings by arguing with them. People with high emotional intelligence won't always feel at ease with their feelings. They may not be in agreement with their feelings however they'll never try to repress them or ignore them. People who are emotionally intelligent will realize how even the most unpleasant of emotions aren't rational. They realize that the use of the logic of "kill off" these emotions is a waste of time which can lead to further frustration.

7.People who have high EQ have the ability effectively say "no" self-control is the highest level of emotional intelligence.Much psychological research has proven that those who struggle with saying no are more likely of suffering from depression, stress and burnout. They also experience anxiety. The art of saying no is a difficult task for us all We don't want to harm others, and we don't want to appear at a negative way in the eyes our spouse, boss or parents. "No" is an expression that has so much power thatwhen used without any explanation and without explanation, people are often confused and astonished. You're not emotional intelligent if you choose to use milder phrases like "I don't think I'm able to", "I'm not sure", "I won't be in a position to" and so on. The people who are emotionally intelligent will use the word "no" whenever they feel they need to say "no" (or "no thanks") and they do not feel the need to justify or justify the reason why they aren't inclined to do something. The end of the story.

Conclusion

Emotional intelligence refers to the ability of a person to recognize and express, manage and analyze one's feelings. Numerous companies have discovered that research has shown that EQ is associated with greater personal success than IQ. Becoming more conscious of your emotions, being flexible in situations of stress as well as reflecting on your previous actions and being aware of the feelings of others are methods to increase your EI. It is essential to develop the ability to use EI when you interact with others within and outside the workplace, and also in personal growth.

www.ingramcontent.com/pod-product-compliance
Lightning Source LLC
Chambersburg PA
CBHW071837080526
44589CB00012B/1022